The Ancien Régime in France

PETER ROBERT CAMPBELL

Basil Blackwell

First published 1988

Basil Blackwell Ltd
108 Cowley Road, Oxford, OX4 1JF, UK

Basil Blackwell Inc.
432 Park Avenue South, Suite 1503
New York, NY 10016, USA

British Library Cataloguing in Publication Data

Campbell, Peter Robert
    The ancien régime in France — (Historical
    Association Studies)
    1. France, 1598–1789
    I. Title
    944'.031

    ISBN 0–631–15107–9

Library of Congress Cataloging in Publication Data

Campbell, Peter (Peter R.)
    The ancien régime in France / Peter Campbell.
        p.   cm. — (Historical association studies)
    ISBN 0–631–15107–9 (pbk.)
    1. France—Politics and government.   2. Monarchy, French—History.
I. Title.   II. Series.
JN2325.C28 1988   88—11620
320.944—dc19   'CIP

Typeset in 9½ on 10 pt Ehrhardt
by Photo·graphics, Honiton, Devon
Printed in Great Britain by Billing & Sons Ltd, Worcester

Contents

Introduction: The Old Orthodoxy

The ancien régime in France may be seen both as a period of history with an ending but no definite starting point, and as a system of government and society. Literally, the term 'ancien régime' means 'former régime', and it was first employed by the French revolutionaries to describe what they hoped to abolish. At first sight, the Revolution of 1789 brought about the final collapse of the old order – but were not many of the characteristics of pre-revolutionary state and society revived under subsequent régimes, and did the Revolution fundamentally alter the economic structures of society? If the Revolution did not constitute a clean break with the past, then when did the ancien régime end? In the nineteenth century?

In truth, the subject of this book is a rather nebulous phenomenon, one which has been defined more in retrospect, by politicians and historians, than by those who lived before the Revolution. The often sophisticated historical, economic, sociological or anthropological theories that we draw upon today to provide us with an explanatory framework were denied to the pre-revolutionary generations. Certainly, they discussed social structures, the legal and political system; they described religious and communal practices, made economic demands (and therefore left a mass of evidence for the historian), but in so doing they revealed to us how very differently they thought. Their concepts are no longer ours, and it requires a great imaginative leap today to see their world in context. The ancien régime is therefore an historical construction and, as successive generations of historians have attempted to analyse it, different features have been emphasized and very different pictures presented. Since the mid nineteenth century, when serious study of the régime began, perspectives have changed and recently historical studies have evolved dramatically. The last two decades in particular have witnessed a proliferation of studies on previously neglected areas. Once, politics and institutions were the main focus of interest, today it seems legitimate to study any and every aspect of the past. To the traditional modern topics such as institutional, financial and social structures, has been added the history of ideologies, popular culture, the rural community,

1

/ards death, the role of women in this patriarchal society, could be extended. New relationships have emerged and problems of synthesis and reinterpretation have to be resolved. is an introduction to the interpretations and debates which centre on the ancien régime, and is one historian's attempt at synthesis.

Early analyses of the ancien régime reflect the growth of historical studies as a discipline. In Restoration France the proximity of the Revolution and bitter political conflict made any attempt at objectivity almost impossible. Properly academic study of the régime only began under the July Monarchy, with archival research and the first publications of historical documents. At this stage, attention was focused upon royal legislative acts, administrative letters and contemporary memoirs. The publication of the latter and the growth of a critical spirit are chronicled in the essays of the great critic Sainte-Beuve, especially in his *Causeries du lundi* (Monday chats) of the 1850s. In 1850 Augustin Thierry published his *Essay on the History of the Formation and Progress of the Third Estate*, which puts forward a view of the development of politics which was to find great favour with contemporaries. In essence, his argument was that the end of feudalism under Louis XI led to the emergence of a new monarchy in alliance with the bourgeoisie. The book was republished several times before the end of the century and not only influenced general views on the steady rise of the bourgeoisie but also determined subsequent research projects. However, the first, and still the most thought-provoking, serious study of the ancien régime is *The Ancien Régime and the Revolution*, published in 1856 by Alexis de Tocqueville. Animated by a liberal desire both to explain the growing centralization in France and to criticize the new despotism of Napoleon III, the book is a profoundly analytical appraisal of the régime from Louis XIV to the Revolution. For Tocqueville the social and judicial institutions of the ancien régime were deeply rooted in the medieval period, whose legacy was one of individualism and a complex archaic network of customs, laws and jurisdictions. But overshadowing all this was the state, whose agents had brought about a centralization of all real power. Thus administrative centralization was the work of the ancien régime monarchy and not of the Revolution. This thesis found wide acceptance, and it seems that, until the 1920s at least, most historians sought to elaborate upon it with detailed studies of individuals and institutions. Voluminous publications of original documents, the works of d'Avenel on the period of Richelieu and Chéruel on the ministry of Colbert all tended in the same direction. Whether by accident or design, the collective *Histoire de France*, edited by Lavisse, embodies a great similarity of perspective on the part of all contributors. This is not surprising, because French historians, until the end of the Third Republic, were the product of the same milieu and education system, and their works generally reflected a liberal confidence in the efficacy of individual actions; hence the numerous biographical studies. Thus, for three or four generations historical studies on the ancien régime broadly followed the pattern established by Tocqueville in 1856. It is fair to say that before the Second World War an orthodoxy had emerged, the product of a remarkably uniform view of history, and of tremendous scholarship. In order to have both a clear chronological idea of our subject and a starting point for subsequent reinterpretations, it is necessary to expound this view in some detail.

For most of these scholars the ancien régime denotes a period of history stretching from the end of the Middle Ages to the French Revolution, characterized by the rise of the centralized modern state. At the end of the fifteenth century the Valois French kings could trace their legitimate line back to the first Capetian monarch in 987. Their domains already included a large part of what we consider France today, but several territories had yet to be acquired. By purchase, escheatment or inheritance, Dauphiné (1456), Burgundy (1447) and Provence (1481) were acquired and Brittany was finally assured in 1532. Although the monarchy had been steadily increasing its power in the thirteenth century, the Hundred Years War had led to the near fragmentation of the kingdom and a tendency towards the development of some independent principalities, as in Languedoc and Brittany. Ultimately, the monarchy had been able to profit sufficiently from its legitimacy and charisma to survive the wars. However, the combined effects of the wartime devastation and recurrent plague left the kingdom drastically weak in the mid fifteenth century. If economic recovery could hardly be effected by the monarchy, it being more a question of a regeneration by local society, political reconstruction was an urgent task. The existence of strong centrifugal and particularist forces, often exploited by powerful princely magnates, made this a supremely difficult task. Nevertheless, the monarchy had emerged from the wars with some significant advantages. It was legitimate, sacred and, after the wars, more prestigious to the extent that it was looked upon with considerable veneration, and even patriotism. Equally important was the right which had been acquired during the previous century of warfare to levy direct taxation, the *taille*. This revenue, combined with that of the extensive royal domains, gave the monarchy both an inestimable financial advantage over rivals for power, and a standing army.

The reigns of Louis XII (1498–1515) and Francis I (1515–47) have been seen as witnessing the consolidation and extension of royal power. Forceful and autocratic personalities, they undertook long and ultimately unsuccessful wars of expansion in Italy. Under Francis I there was a notable development and reorganization of royal finance, made necessary by the frequent wars. Nevertheless, ordinary revenue being insufficient, recourse was had to sale of office, loans and indirect taxes, all the fiscal expedients that were destined to become such a feature of hard-pressed royal finances for the next two centuries. Control over the church was regularized by the Concordat of Bologna in 1516 and a vast source of

3

royal patronage assured for the future. Royal legislative authority was developed and exercised by the codification of customary laws and an important series of ordinances in 1536–9. The edict of Villers–Cotterets (1539) saw the extension of French as the administrative language for the whole state. Progress continued during the reign of Henri II (1547–59) when a new layer of courts was established; these were the presidial courts, and they formed an intermediate level between the senechalcies and the parlements.

Thus from the mid sixteenth century it is possible to discern the essential structures of the absolute monarchy both administratively and institutionally. Notwithstanding, royal power in this period was far from being efficient or truly bureaucratic. It depended upon household government, in the form of an itinerant court (to impress the realm with the presence of the prince) and a compromise with magnate power and provincial and corporate liberties. Seyssel, describing the *Grande Monarchie de France* in 1515, considered its power to be bridled by three checks: religion (the monarch's duty to behave as a good Christian), *police* (the need to respect all previous edicts and regulations) and justice (the courts). The Renaissance monarchy was therefore a limited monarchy which was developing more bureaucratic and authoritarian characteristics.

However, the progress of the monarchy was to be rudely interrupted by a long period of instability. The onset of a regency (under Catherine de Medici) and of religious quarrels between Catholics and Protestants ushered in a period of recurrent civil war which was to last until almost the end of the century. Factional and religious conflict brought the prestige of the monarchy to a very low ebb. This period saw renewed devastation, the elaboration of doctrines of resistance to royal power, including theories of tyrannicide, and a recrudescence of the power of the magnates. The last, as leading courtiers and royal provincial governors, were able to develop dangerously independent power bases in the provinces.

Fortunately for the monarchy, the last decade of the reign of Henri IV (1589–1610) was another time of recovery and reconstruction. By military victory and a shrewd conversion to Catholicism this first Bourbon king preserved the principles of legitimacy and Catholicism for the French monarchy. The Edict of Nantes (1598) guaranteed the freedom of Protestant worship wherever it already existed, except in Paris and a few other towns, and gave the Huguenots legal guarantees and approximately one hundred secure places. Under the supervision of Sully, order was temporarily brought into the finances without any new departures. Trade was subjected to increased regulation and the monetary preoccupations of the monarchy are revealed in the development of what historians would later call a mercantilist policy. The previous demands of royal finance meant that by this period almost all judicial, fiscal and courtly offices were venal, and this system was further regularized by the *paulette* of 1604. This was an annual tax paid by office-holders which

4

gave them the right to bequeath their office to a chosen successor, subject only to the royal veto on the grounds of real unsuitability. The hereditary aspect of the royal bureaucracy was thus immeasurably strengthened, and local office-holders were tied more securely to the monarchy. When Henry IV was assassinated by a Catholic fanatic in 1610 the power and prestige of the monarchy had been restored.

The Cardinal de Richelieu, who was in power from 1624 until 1642, has been seen as the early architect of 'absolutism' in France. As first minister of Louis XIII (1610–43), he subordinated internal policy to the exigencies of a foreign policy directed against the Habsburgs. To diplomatic and financial participation in the Thirty Years War from the 1620s, military intervention was added from 1635. This required unprecedented large supplies of money from a population living mainly at a subsistence level, and subject to plague and famine at a time when the French economy was just beginning a century-long depression. The situation was desperate and the ministry struggled to mobilize resources. A strong sense of royal majesty, a certain concept of the state, the fiscal requirements of foreign policy, the need for order and obedience, all these led to administrative change and royal propaganda on a previously unprecedented scale. After 1635, the weight of direct taxation increased dramatically and the value of other fiscal expedients even more so. This, more than any other, was a period of stresses and strains which brought about significant developments in the monarchical system.

From this period the use of royal intendants with commissions revocable at will became general. Extensive powers were conferred upon them to promote the efficiency of the royal fiscal system, and they tended to become permanent agents in the provinces. It is argued that as government became more specialized, there was a greater reliance upon professional bureaucrats and less recourse to the higher nobility and princes of the blood, who regarded themselves as the king's natural counsellors. The composition of the council of state reflected this tendency and the independence of the governors is supposed to have been reduced by the intendants. On these grounds historians have claimed that the monarchy relied more upon the new bourgeois office-holders and less upon the old aristocracy. In this view there was thus a shift in the social basis of the state during the first half of the seventeenth century.

At every level of French society, dominated as it was by the concepts of provincial liberty, tradition, precedent, privilege and immunity, there was resistance and non-cooperation. Peasant revolts became endemic from about 1630, the provincial administrations, especially the courts, became increasingly unmanageable, and the princes ever more resentful of royal policy. During the regency of Anne of Austria, when power was in the hands of Cardinal Mazarin, the continuation of war and fiscal expedients, now affecting all levels of society, eventually provoked a crisis. In 1648 the Paris parlement finally attempted to prevent further exactions and constitutional innovations. A particular and successful demand was the abolition of those hated royal agents, the intendants, who had usurped the powers of so many local officials. A compromise was reached with Mazarin's government but when the cardinal tried to retaliate and the princes of the blood became involved, civil war broke out. The wars lasted until 1653 and renewed devastation resulted, although this time it was more localized. The regions of Bordeaux and Paris suffered particularly badly. The Fronde has usually been interpreted as a combination of the last fling of the magnates with the traditionalist resistance of a venal bureaucracy. In this view it therefore represents a decisive stage in the development of 'absolute' monarchy, for, it is said, the royal victory ultimately opened the path to renewed government centralization during the personal rule of Louis XIV. (But see below, pp. 54–70.)

'Colbert is universally regarded as the organizer of the administrative monarchy', wrote Georges Pagès, one of France's most distinguished institutional historians in 1932. At first the re-established intendants were primarily to be observers and they were warned against undue interference with the local corps of officers, but with the onset of wars after 1672 they gradually acquired ever wider functions. Once permanently installed in the provinces they exploited their judicial and financial commissions to become veritable royal administrators, who were accountable only to the royal council. The final stage in their development was the virtual annihilation of local independence by their powers to regulate the problems of municipal and communal debts. 'Thus around 1680, the last obstacle capable of preventing the establishment of an administrative monarchy disappeared and the long evolution, which began perhaps a century before and resulted in the creation of a centralized administration in France, was complete.' The reorganization of the army by Le Tellier and Louvois and the reduction of the recalcitrant parlements to obedience (1673) paralleled other developments in the administration. In an influential article Pagès summarized his views:

> For a long time foreign and civil war prevented the king's ministers from further pursuing the reform of the interior. For a long time the role of the intendant of justice, *police* and finance remained ill-defined; he was something between a straightforward commissioner extraordinary and permanent delegate of royal power. The administrative transformation, which would sooner or later be the inevitable consequence of their continued presence in the provinces, only took place, or so it seems, after the restoration of peace, during the ministry of Colbert. Whether Colbert intended it or not . . . administrative centralization, of which the intendants were the principal agents, was to be the result of, and indeed did result from, the restoration of order, the organization of the *police* and the tutelage imposed upon the communities. This was the last

form of administrative organization in ancien régime France, and was to last until the Revolution. (Pagés, 1932a)

According to this traditional view, the personal rule of Louis XIV was therefore the apogee of the ancien régime and this was symbolized by the permanent installation of the court in the château of Versailles in 1682. Here the political power of the higher nobility was finally curtailed as court life reduced them to dependence upon the king. Royal *gloire* and French culture radiated over France and much of Europe, establishing the kingdom as a cultural and political model for other rulers. But Louis's search for *gloire* and the need to play a forceful role in European politics resulted in almost constant involvement in foreign war until nearly the end of the reign. The later period therefore saw renewed recourse to the old fiscal expedients, now on a greater scale than ever. Worse, the revocation of the Edict of Nantes in 1685 had been conceived of as the final establishment of religious uniformity, but it proved to be economically and politically harmful as 300,000 Protestants went into exile. The result was the 'warping' of the régime and the growth of serious criticism of royal despotism, chiefly written by exiled Huguenots and by the aristocratic entourage of the heir presumptive to the throne, the Duc de Bourgogne. When Louis XIV died in 1715 France was exhausted after the long wars, the monarchy was endebted to the tune of 2,000 million *livres* and the parlements were resisting royal policy over the Jansenists.

Nevertheless, the personal rule of Louis XIV so impressed historians and contemporaries alike that until recently it has been hard to regard the subsequent rulers as anything more than inadequate copies. The following three-quarters of a century has therefore been seen as a period of steady decline of the old régime, whose decay was punctuated by intermittent and unsuccessful attempts at reform. The Regency of d'Orléans was marked by an unsuccessful revival of aristocratic government during the experiment of the Polysynodie (1715–18) and the resurgence of the power and opposition of the Paris parlement. A serious attempt at the establishment of government credit and a state bank under the direction of John Law came to a disastrous end with the spectacular collapse of confidence in its shares in 1720. Although John Law's system has been extensively studied, the following thirty years have been much neglected by historians. The short ministry of the Duc de Bourbon (1723–6) attempted an unsuccessful fiscal reform which was doomed by factional intrigue. The long years of ascendancy of the Cardinal de Fleury (1726–43) have generally been regarded as no more than a phase of slow economic recovery after both the wars of Louis XIV and the financial difficulties left unsolved by the Regency. After the cardinal's death in 1743, Louis XV (1715–75) briefly attempted to succeed Fleury as active head of his own ministry, but his lack of resolution led to the proliferation of factions, operating through the influence of royal mistresses, and to the increased independence of the secretaries of state. This was the age of Madame de Pompadour and Madame du Barry.

The dubious thesis that there was a regrouping of the aristocracy in the first half of the century under the leadership of the parlementaires and aided by the enlightened political theories of Montesquieu, has been widely accepted. The focal point of opposition to absolutism was identified as the Paris parlement which, from the 1730s, engaged in a running battle with the ministry over religious policy and ministerial despotism. In 1762 it succeeded in having the Jesuits expelled from France on the grounds of their 'despotic' organization. In the mid 1760s the parlement of Brittany attempted to impeach the royal provincial governor, the Duc d'Aiguillon, and its cause was espoused by the Paris parlement, with dramatic consequences. Many historians have regarded the Brittany affair as the beginning of the end of the régime. It led to the defeat of Choiseul's faction and the complete abolition and reorganization of the parlements in 1771. This confirmed in the eyes of many observers what they had long feared, namely that the absolute monarchy had become despotic.

The reign of Louis XVI (1774–92) began with the recall of the old parlement and a reforming ministry led by Turgot, who was soon out of office. Once again, reform was frustrated by vested interests, courtly faction and the deeply rooted structures of the régime. Yet, the times were changing, war was ever more expensive and reform ever more necessary.

Perhaps the final act of the régime began with intervention in the American War of Independence in 1778. The reforms of the finance minister Necker were left unfinished and the war paid for by large-scale borrowing. After the war the interest on the royal debt amounted to nearly half of the annual revenue. In the absence of a sound credit system, reform of the royal finances was now imperative.

There were several reasons why reform plans should have provoked a serious political crisis. First, the fiscal system was closely related to the social system in that fiscal exemptions were largely possessed by those of superior social rank. A reorganization of the system would run up against the powerful vested interests of the nobility and clergy at court and in the provinces. In addition, the maintenance of public confidence in royal loans, the political theory of the monarchy and the widespread public belief in 'constitutionalism' did not allow the government to impose reforms of a fundamental nature without first having consulted some form of representative assembly. If such an assembly met it would be difficult for the ministry to ignore the expression of grievances. The controller-general Calonne, therefore, presented his views to an Assembly of Notables in 1787, at which he not only failed to have his projects accepted but he also revealed the disastrous state of the royal finances, inadvertently opening public debate on the nature and extent of reform. Over the next year aristocratic and parlementaire resistance to the reforming ministry was able to exploit the need for confidence for the floating of government loans in order to bring about the calling of the Estates General, a national representative institution which had last met in 1614. The French monarchy was facing its most serious crisis.

Public debate on the form of the Estates General and the democratic nature of the electoral process served greatly to raise the political temperature in France. To make matters worse, the economic crisis of the 1780s was at its height, with a bad harvest in 1788. The need for wholesale reform was widely recognized, and by May 1789 the bourgeoisie was beginning to assert itself in the provinces and popular disorders were breaking out. Many radicals were plainly expecting a greater attack on the system of privilege – which would be a blow at the very roots of the political and social structure of the ancien régime – than many nobles or churchmen were prepared to consider. The failure of the monarchy to provide a strong lead in the Estates General from May until June 1789 led to exasperation and the final seizure of the initiative by the Third Estate, which was composed principally of members of the bourgeoisie. The popular disorders and serious disaffection in the army meant that Louis XVI had no choice but to acquiesce in the victory of the Third Estate over the recalcitrant elements of the other two. The fall of the Bastille on 14 July 1789 symbolized this victory. It was then clear that the assembly would itself undertake the task of reform and draw up a constitution for France. Thus, in the summer of 1789 the civil disorders and the political revolution ensured the collapse of the ancien régime. Three years later the thousand-year-old monarchy was abolished and shortly thereafter the king executed. The history of the former régime could begin to be written.

A history of the evolution of political and constitutional ideas has been integrated with this view of the political development of the ancien régime. The sacred character of the French monarchy can be traced back to the coronation of Charlemagne in Rome in AD800. This theocratic aspect was repeatedly emphasized both in the coronation ceremony and by the popular belief in the king's ability to cure scrofula by touch. According to St Paul, and subsequently a whole tradition of political Augustinianism, temporal authority was derived from God. The king was seen as a judge who owed justice and order to his subjects. Early in the history of the state the power of the monarchy was diminished by checks implicit in the feudal system of relations. Corporations and estates largely organized their own *police* and consultation with local or national assemblies developed as a result of the financial needs of the monarchy. Many areas had provincial assemblies by the end of the fifteenth century, but they never acquired such power as to justify a description of France as a *ständesstaat*, a state of estates. The term 'medieval constitutionalism' may be used to describe the idea that checks, consultation and comment were an integral part of the working of the state. However, from the thirteenth century quarrels between the Empire

9

and the Papacy led to the exploitation of the Roman concept of imperialism which emphasized the independence of the ruler from external authorities. The maxim 'the king is emperor in his own kingdom' was employed in that sense. This shift to Roman law by jurists was to be combined with new ideas of the state at the end of the Middle Ages to lead to the exaltation of the legislative authority of the ruler at the expense of lesser authorities. Such was the situation at the beginning of the sixteenth century, as it is so lucidly described by Seyssel.

According to traditional histories of political thought, the next important development came with Bodin's *Six Books of the Republic* (1576). In the debate over the extent of royal power during the civil wars, it expresses a moderate viewpoint. Bodin is often regarded as the first theoretician of absolute monarchy, on the grounds that he defined sovereignty as it was to be exploited by royalists later. However, the civil wars of the late sixteenth century gave rise to numerous tracts and pamphlets on political thought, most of which were themselves justifications for the more extreme Protestant or Catholic attitudes to the monarchy. The theoretical basis of monarchical power was explored in works which drew on medieval constitutionalism, with contractual theories and notions of popular sovereignty. Such theories were in contradiction with the theological and Roman defences of authority expounded by the royal jurists, and they were potentially extremely dangerous for the monarchy. Censorship and the reassertion of monarchical power under Henri IV and his successors ensured that they ceased to have common currency.

Richelieu and his propagandists are credited with the next significant step. The idea of *raison d'état* was a valuable and more modern support for older beliefs in the wide royal prerogative to act in the interest of the commonwealth. However, it was again the reign of Louis XIV which saw the apogee of the theory of absolute monarchy. Historians recognize that absolute monarchy never entirely freed itself from all restraints to act, but in this period the extreme claims of the lawyers were becoming commonplaces of political theory. The most masterly exposition and defence of divine right theories on behalf of the monarchy, is the *Politics taken from the very words of the Holy Scriptures*, by Bishop Bossuet (1709). It seemed hardly possible to go further than Bossuet in praise and justification of wisely used sovereign power in the interests of order. The book is certainly the most quoted work on the theory of absolute monarchy. Another work often cited is *The Sighs of France Enslaved*, written by an exiled Protestant in 1689. It paints a very different picture of the monarchy and may be said to have begun the attack on Louis XIV. Unfortunately, the opposition theories of the Circle of the Duc de Bourgogne (whose members included Fénelon, Vauban, Boulainvilliers and Saint-Simon) are often still dismissed by historians as reactionary apologia for the aristocracy. In fact, there was much that was new in their ideas and they were influential in the eighteenth century.

In an important paper published in 1955, Professors Mousnier and

Hartung argued that in its essentials the theory of absolute monarchy remained remarkably consistent from the beginning of the sixteenth century until the middle of the eighteenth century. Basing their conclusions more on the theory than the practice of the monarchy (for research in that area had yet to be done) they defined absolute monarchy as a 'monarchy limited by divine law and national law', which enjoyed wide prerogatives to preserve the commonwealth, but which was not despotic. 'This notion of absolutism oscillates around a point of equilibrium, between the conception of a power less limited and that of a power which was more limited.' In keeping with this view numerous historians consider that the ancien régime monarchy had a constitution, albeit an unwritten one, which precluded the tyrannical exercise of power. Such a view has been most eloquently expressed by Michel Antoine:

> It is certain that in the eyes of the French the nation had a constitution, a 'customary constitution, derived from the vital necessities of the body politic, in which the king was the head and the subjects the members. This constitution was beyond the royal will'. But the fluctuations, the uncertainties, the fashions in the interpretation of the limits of royal authority brought variety and change to its daily exercise. They modified the immutable aspect of the great principles and thus gave the constitution of the kingdom its specific quality of a customary constitution, replete with contradictions. Did they not declare that the king's sovereignty was unlimited, and at the same time limited? That the prince was beneath the law, but was also above it? That he should appoint magistrates, but always retained the possibility of passing judgment himself? Although they may at first seem disconcerting, these contradictions were in reality a vital part of the constitution, which survived only to the extent that no attempt was made to resolve them. The régime was thus based upon principles which could be maintained only if they were not pushed to their logical conclusion.
> (Antoine, p. 31)

The fact is that, if France had a constitution, it was an extremely nebulous and ill-defined one, to the extent that controversy over its nature not only exists today but also existed during the ancien régime.

If the development of political theory paralleled the development of the state, ideologies also played a part in its decline and overthrow. Indeed, they now took on a more active role, since it is often said that before the eighteenth century events preceded ideas, whereas the reverse was true later. From the mid eighteenth century the Enlightenment provided an ideology of resistance to the ancien régime. The spirit of rational criticism undermined the religious basis of the monarchy and also exposed the injustices and shortcomings of royal policies. The essentially liberal and humanitarian theories of the Enlightenment are

11

thought to have played a key role in sapping the foundations of the monarchy. A modern world view was replacing the antiquated traditionalism of the French political and social system. The new ideas were widely diffused amongst the upper echelons of society and they found their way down the social scale thanks to the influence of the gutter press and the indiscreet criticisms of the ministry, replete with Montesquieuan notions, contained in the remonstrances which the parlements had taken to publishing. The intellectual origins of the bourgeois revolution are therefore to be found in the Enlightenment: were not the leading philosophers idolized by the revolutionaries? Thus the history of political thought accords well with standard views on the origins of the Revolution.

Furthermore, the principal stages of the social and economic history of the three centuries also neatly fitted the overall view. There were, of course, local studies of rural or urban societies, but they were rarely made into the foundations of the picture. The main focus of attention was the rise of capitalism and the effect of economic policy. In particular, the transition from feudalism to capitalism has been called upon as an explanatory device for political events. As the régime was so deeply rooted in medieval society it was unlikely to prove sufficiently adaptable to negotiate this transition successfully, especially if it relied too heavily upon the feudal order of nobility. A certain view of the characteristics and role of the nobility and the bourgeoisie has therefore prevailed. The former have been seen as virtually a caste, parasitic and non-adaptable, while the latter represented developing commercialism and progressive ways of thinking. The economic expansion of the sixteenth century was extremely favourable to the development of commerce, and therefore of the bourgeoisie, and the prolonged rise in prices over the same period had a disastrous impact upon the nobility, we are told. Arguing mainly from literary evidence which reflects the nobles' perception of themselves, many historians have maintained that there was a decline in the wealth of the old nobility owing to the effects of the price revolution on the fixed rents and dues paid to the seigneurs. At the same time, seigneuries and royal offices were being bought up by a rising merchant class. By the first half of the seventeenth century the nobility was, therefore, experiencing not only a political crisis of influence but also an economic one. However, the long depression of the seventeenth century saw a drain of merchant capital into investments in land, state finances and offices. The bourgeoisie failed to develop a consciousness and opted for a traditional value system orientated towards the acquisition of nobility. This postponed development had enabled the monarchy to emerge preeminent as a strong force in its own right. However, the renewed and rapid commercial expansion from the 1720s created a larger and more demanding class of bourgeoisie over the next half-century. This increasingly self-conscious group was prevented from acquiring political power by the so-called aristocratic reaction, which manifested itself in the political, social and seigneurial sphere. At the same time, the

12

bourgeoisie was hampered in its development by the survival of arch
customs, state regulations and a burdensome system of internal tar...
barriers which the aristocratic state could do little to change. Given no
share of political power and paying more in taxes than the privileged
aristocracy, the bourgeoisie became increasingly hostile to the ancien
régime./The French Revolution was the inevitable consequence of these
tensions in a society in transition./The seizure of power by the bourgeoisie
gave it a chance to enact the Enlightenment philosophy of liberty, and
one result was the abolition of the restrictions on the liberty of the
individual and of commerce. The argument is all too neat.

Thus in its outlines, the social, intellectual and political history of the
ancien régime formed a single intellectual structure. This orthodoxy
possesses a unity of perspective and of focus. Yet this has not prevented
debate on some major issues. Within this general framework historians
on the Right and Left have evaluated the régime quite differently. Their
views usually depend upon contrasting the ancien régime with the
revolutionary régimes which succeeded it and which became the basis
of French society and politics during the nineteenth century and after.
The Right, which for a long time refused to accept the permanence of
the Revolution, has usually found much to admire in the old régime,
especially during its seventeenth-century phase. From Taine until the
present day, a somewhat idealized image has been put forward, in which
the existence of a stable society of orders is emphasized. The accent is
put upon the family, reciprocal relations between seigneur and peasant,
the sense of hierarchy and order, all of which may be juxtaposed with
the disorders of revolutionary society. The image of the seventeenth
century as a great age of *gloire* and the rise of the powerful nation state
was drawn in the light of the defeat of France in 1870 and the powerful
sentiment of French nationalism that subsequently arose. The intellectual
climate of Action Française glorified monarchy, and it was after the
Popular Front (1936) and during the Vichy régime that research was
published on the corporate society of the ancien régime. Perhaps Georges
Lefebvre was right to suggest (in the 1950s) that the attack on the social
interpretation of the Revolution owed as much to fear of social revolution
during the Cold War as it did to scholarship. Historians on the Right,
therefore, paint a more favourable picture of state and society in the
century before the Revolution. On the other hand, liberals, or those
further to the Left, have, from 1789 onwards, tended to highlight the
injustices of the régime, pointing to the system of privilege, the lack of
individual liberty and the sometimes despotic exercise of royal power.
For many Marxists the ancien régime was, and still continues to be
regarded as, essentially a feudal society which produced a certain form
of the state, the absolute monarchy, to defend its interests.

For scholars, the period studied has also often been determined by
political inclinations. Whereas historians on the Right have tended to

concentrate upon the political régime in the Grand Siècle, the Left has, because of its socialist revolutionary tradition, focused upon the Revolution and its origins. For this reason the orthodox view of the origins of the Revolution emphasizes social and economic change in society. What is perhaps surprising is that this Marxist perspective has been accepted even by the Right, such that everyone seemed to agree on the 'bourgeois' revolution. The Rightists' view of a stable, ordered society has had to be tailored to fit this orthodoxy on 1789. This is done by characterizing the period after about 1750 as an era of more rapid transformation of social and economic relations.

Orthodoxies can be insidiously pervasive in historical studies. They provide a ready-made guide to the period which weaves a path through the awful complexities lying in wait for the unwary beginner, and as such are useful. But by their nature they are difficult to attack, because criticism in one area provokes a response buttressed by other parts of the well-integrated overall structure. Since it would be illegitimate to generalize from too particular an area, and since nobody can master all old and new research in the collective enterprise that is history, the edifice is left standing while columns have been replaced. The nature of the French university system has also played a part, for it was rooted in the nineteenth century and favoured the dominance by great professors over research projects and the teaching syllabus. Perhaps only by the 1970s had there been a sufficient accumulation of critical material to make possible revision in most areas of this orthodoxy.

Indeed, as an interpretation of the ancien régime, it leaves much to be desired. The perspective is centred far too much upon the origins of the nineteenth-century state and on great individuals, and far too little upon the context in which both individual and state operated. And yet, as Guenée (1964) has argued, the social history of the state should be an essential component of its history: the way an office-holder conceives of his task is just as important as the ordinances that define it; important too are the material conditions in which he operates, from the state of communications to the availability of clerks and aides. However, although it is still possible and necessary to breathe new life into old subjects, much more significant are the new departures which have been made under the influence of a new philosophy of history since the 1920s. A new school of historians has grown up in France, with parallels in the United States and Britain, which has evolved new concepts of the appropriate subjects to study and new ways of defining their perimeters. Rejecting the compartmentalization of the social sciences and the traditionalism of history, the Annales School has paid particular attention to social groups and short- and long-term movements in the economy. Studying regions over perhaps two centuries, which is a long enough timespan to include a long-term cycle in the economy (as Le Roy Ladurie has done for *The Peasants of Languedoc*, or Goubert on *Beauvais and the Beauvaisis*), they have generated a new understanding of ancien régime

France. The whole perspective has changed, for now the context of the state has been so thoroughly explored that the framework of explanation itself has altered. Without denying the important effects of religion and the state upon society, it can be argued that the basis of the whole system lay in the rural economy and the demography of peasant society. Equally exciting are the enormous advances that have been made in the understanding of cultural factors, especially the belief system of the popular classes. The following chapters have been written in the light of this new approach. They should be read as a dialogue with the established views that have been outlined above.

It is appropriate to begin with the economy and social basis of society before moving on to discuss the patterns of belief. The political and administrative system will then be set in the broadest possible context.

1 Economy and Society

Walking up a long hill, to ease my mare, I was joined by a poor woman who complained of the times, and that it was a sad country; demanding her reasons, she said her husband had but a morsel of land, one cow, and a poor little horse, yet they had a *franchar* (42 lb) of wheat and three chickens to pay as quit rent to one seigneur; and four *franchar* of oats, one chicken and 1 sou to pay to another, besides very heavy tailles and other taxes. She had seven children, and the cow's milk helped to make the soup ... This woman, at no great distance, might have been taken for sixty or seventy, her figure was so bent, and her face so furrowed and hardened by labour, but she said she was only twenty-eight.

This portrait of a peasant woman taken from Arthur Young's *Travels in France* in 1789 was not an inaccurate one. Her situation represents the degradation of the condition of the French peasant since the early sixteenth century, although she seems a little better off than the 'poor animals' described by La Bruyère or Vauban during the terrible epoch of Louis XIV. This woman would have lived in a one-roomed house with a cellar below it and a yard where vegetables grew and the poultry ran. The house might have been built of stone, or quite probably of mud; it was possibly windowless (there was a tax on windows) and had a thatched roof if it was in a grain-producing area or a tiled one if in a vine area. More likely than not her husband would not have owned the poor dwelling, for it would have been rented from either a richer member of the village community or a townsman. On the floor of beaten mud covered with straw would have been a bed, which was usually far and away the most expensive item a peasant owned. Parents and children probably all slept in it in order to protect themselves from the wintry cold. To judge from inventories after death, the other furniture would not have amounted to much. There would have been a chest, a table and some stools, a few books of devotion and probably little else besides some cooking implements and the fireplace.

The woman's miserable peasant existence would probably not have lasted for more than another ten years, on average, for it has been calculated that having reached twenty a person might expect to live only until the late thirties. In fact, she would have been fortunate to reach marrying age, because infant mortality was very high throughout this period – only half of those born reached twenty. Nearly one-quarter of all babies died before the end of their first year and a quarter of the survivors before the age of five. These children died of smallpox, measles and other contagious diseases, and especially of digestive illnesses – dysentry, for example, was endemic. Family record books constantly contain cryptic references such as 'And the said child died one year and a half later'. In 1534 the three-year-old son of a provincial noble died: 'the aforesaid child died of smallpox which was wondrous common at that time and which made his eye all pustulous, then during a cold his teeth fell from his mouth and he died and so did others of the said pox'.

Arthur Young's peasant woman probably would not have given birth to seven children by twenty-eight even if she had married very young, so it is almost certain that she had married a widower who already had children. Around 1700 in the Paris basin the average age of marriage was $24\frac{1}{2}$ for women and $26\frac{1}{2}$ for men. This represents a probable increase since the fourteenth century, and in the sixteenth century it was 20 for women and 24 for men. By the late eighteenth century the age had increased to $26\frac{1}{2}$ for women and $28\frac{1}{2}$ for men. We shall return to the reason for this rise later in the chapter. Because mortality was so high, and life expectancy so short, remarriages were frequent in all classes of society, for one partner would often die much earlier than the other. Widowers found it easier to remarry than widows, especially as they got older. Jacques Quentin Durand, of Rethel in Champagne, was a notary born in 1719. He married his first wife in 1744, when he was thirty-four. He lived happily with her for six months, at the end of which time she caught a fever and died. A year later he remarried, but this wife died in childbirth. His description of her is well worth quoting for several reasons: it reveals his idea of a virtuous wife, the practice of marrying someone of similar social standing, the preoccupation with salvation and the poor quality of medical practices.

She was only seventeen and a half when she died; she had a well formed mind, was quite against coquetry and finery, devoted to her husband, sensible, endowed with a respectable fortune and descended from a very honorable family in the town; she had only received extreme unction, but she died just a week after having been to confession and communion. I am greatly sorry that they did not pull out the baby in pieces and I wish they hadn't bled her because in that event she would not have been so exhausted and might have been saved; but her uncle the doctor having ordered all that was done, she could not have been in the hands of anyone more interested in her preservation; such a perfect union ruptured by this woeful death, has plunged me into the deepest grief.

17

Durand married again, however, fifteen months later and this time all went well. Over the next fourteen years his wife gave birth to five children (more or less the average number of births per marriage throughout this period) of whom three died within two years of their birth.

A slightly higher death rate for children in the towns was due partly to wet nursing, which became a widespread practice in the eighteenth century. Babies would be sent to peasant mothers in the countryside for their first twenty months, where negligence and poor hygiene took its toll. An extraordinarily high proportion of them died: in Rouen the death rate was double that of children nursed by their mothers, reaching 38 per cent of them. Foundlings had even less chance of survival: around 85 per cent of them did not live beyond their fifth year. A high death rate was constant for very young children, but older sectors of the population tended to be carried off by death in great swathes. These periods are known by French historians as *mortalités*. Although there was tremendous regional variation in the incidence of *mortalités*, few of which affected the whole kingdom at once, the general causes are easy to discern. An undernourished population living in unhygienic conditions and dependent on polluted water was already a good target for disease and death. It used to be thought that famine was the prime cause, but research has shown that high bread prices as a result of shortage could exist without a *mortalité*. Successive poor harvests, however, would reduce the resistance of the population and make it more susceptible to disease. Dysentry and plague were great scourges (although the plague mysteriously disappeared around 1670), and war was another. In 1667 the French army was in the Lille region, pillaging and burning. 'All the peasants were trying to save everything in their homes and all the church ornaments. It was a great calamity, to see the poor peasants running all about to put their belongings in the towns.' The documents are full of the extreme disorder of soldiers, who regularly left a trail of devastation behind them even if they were French and in their own country. In fact, war meant plague, because the soldiers carried disease with them. In 1628 Richelieu sent a relief force from La Rochelle to northern Italy, and during its passage across southern France it spread a plague which carried off more than a million people. This was quite exceptional, and there were no such widespread disasters thereafter, but more localized cases remained frequent. Epidemics ensured that the population of Brittany declined in the eighteenth century, in a period when the population was generally increasing in France.

This sort of information was not available to historians before the 1960s, for demography is a new science. Methods of family reconstitution were devised in the 1950s, and a systematic consultation of documents then followed. The calculations are still imprecise and approximate, especially on mortality, because of the lack of records in a pre-statistical era. Births, marriages and deaths were not entirely satisfactorily recorded throughout the period and hardly at all in the sixteenth century. Only

18

after 1676 are there anything like reasonable statistics to work with. In addition, we should never forget the existence of regional variations owing to differences of habitat, diet, climate and the incidence of warfare. However, the basic demographic rules that governed France did not change throughout the ancien régime.

For all the precariousness of individual lives, France was the most heavily populated country in Europe throughout the period. This is true whether we speak of the mid sixteenth century, when the population was, at a rough estimate, some 18 million (in a smaller area than later), or the 22 million in 1710, or the 27–8 million of 1789. The population increase over these centuries, and especially during the eighteenth, does not appear to have been produced by a vital revolution or an agricultural revolution; rather it was the fruit of a steady tendency to growth (around 3 per cent per annum) which had suffered periodic checks by *mortalités* during a long seventeenth century (1560–1720). After each *mortalité* the population usually regained its previous level remarkably quickly and began to increase again.

The mass of the population lived in the countryside, and most lived in small villages. According to Dupâquier, in the Paris basin, even including the enormous town of Paris, 70 per cent of peasants lived in parishes containing less than 300 households and four-fifths of these lived in villages of less than 200 households. 'Thus at least 70% of the inhabitants of the Paris Basin could put a name to the face of everyone they met; in turn they themselves were known and recognised. They would meet at church, at weddings, feasts, wakes, and perhaps at charivaris. They helped one another, watched one another. A network of relationships, kinships, friendships and hostilities bound together each village.' The village functioned as an economic and social unit, not without its divisions of course, but the solidarity created by having communal patterns of cultivation, by being in the same parish and often in the same seigneurie, and by having collective responsibility for taxes, was a strong one. The great grain-producing plains of the north-east were cultivated in huge fields in which peasants owned small plots, and the open-field model was repeated in other areas. The two- or three-field system of rotation was usual and a field might lie fallow for one or several years before being ploughed again. Agricultural techniques had barely changed since the Middle Ages and they were primitive. Wooden ploughs were used, sowing was by hand, and so, of course, was harvesting. Fertilizers, except for manure, were either unknown or too expensive to transport, and the manure produced by the scrawny, undernourished livestock (which competed for grain with humans so could not be given much) was insufficient. Grain was grown wherever it was possible to do so. The quality of the seed was poor and yields were low. They varied from area to area, of course, according to the soil, but were on average about 6 to 1, and less in a bad year.

The logic of the agricultural economy goes a long way to explain the

19

condition of the peasantry. According to Pierre Goubert, it took about 20 hectolitres of grain to feed a family of six people. This would grow in four acres, but as only one-third could be sown in any year, 12 acres of property would be needed. The peasant would have to keep back at least one-sixth of his crop for the next year's seed, the product of another two-thirds of an acre of sown land. Thus, before any dues or taxes were subtracted, the peasant would have needed to own about 14 acres of land to be sufficient in corn. However, he had to pay dues to the seigneur and taxes to the state which were increasingly heavy during the seventeenth century. The church tithe reduced his income further and so did the parish. Seigneurial and clerical dues were often levied in kind at harvest time, the church taking about 1 bushel in 12, and the seigneur the same, although seigneurial dues could be very light in some areas and very heavy in others. The state might take as much as 20 per cent of the peasant's income by 1700, and the parish about 4 per cent. Thus, nearly 40 per cent of the peasant's income in grain went to someone else. The peasant needed to own twice as much land, about 25 acres, to feed his family in a good year. Unfortunately, the peasantry did not own much of the land it cultivated in France. The church, the nobility and the urban bourgeoisie owned a good deal which they rented out to the peasant for cultivation, who therefore needed an even larger farm. The terms varied a lot, but land was usually either leased for a number of years at a fixed rent, or let out on a sharecropping basis. The latter, known as *métairie*, became increasingly popular with landowners from the fifteenth century. Louis Merle has studied the system in Poitou, where it expanded rapidly in the first half of the sixteenth century and more slowly for the next century and a half. Smaller plots of land were grouped together and let out for five years in return for a percentage of the crop. By the late seventeenth century the percentage was almost always 50 per cent and the tenancy seven years. *Métayage* became general in the southern half of France. Gradually the grouping of plots of land into larger units for renting changed the landscape, as *bocage* – smaller enclosed fields with hedges or boundaries to mark the end of the property – became more generalized. The peasant needed to cultivate a great deal more land if he rented it than if he owned it.

The fundamental problem was that three-quarters of all peasants owned too little land to enable them to be self-sufficient. Most worked only a few acres and rented the rest, but this too was insufficient, so they had recourse to other forms of income. The yard was cultivated, a few animals would graze on the common or fallow lands, the householder would sell his labour, and that of his sons also, on a daily basis to a richer peasant or the seigneur. He might have a second occupation as a village artisan, woodcutter or ditcher, and in the slack season of the agricultural year other employment might be found in the form of cottage industries, especially textiles. Sons and daughters would be sent into domestic service in their teens, either with a richer farmer or in the local town, and this meant fewer mouths to feed and perhaps some additional income. Thus, daughters could save for their dowries and sons survive until they inherited enough land to set up home and take a wife. The inheritance customs also played a part in exacerbating the land question. Different laws and customs prevailed in different localities – Roman law generally in the south and customary law in the north – but where primogeniture was practised other sons were left with very little, and where there was a custom of equal shares among sons the subdivision of holdings took place even more rapidly. Marriage strategies would counterbalance this tendency, but it is true that there was a 'proletarianization' of the peasantry during the period.

It has been assumed that the failure to develop more sophisticated farming techniques, the immobility of the peasant world, was due to the weight of centuries of empiricism. A report from a society of agriculture expressed it thus: 'usually they have only routines, but this term need not necessarily imply ineptitude. More than once we have had occasion to remark that certain rural practices, which appear to be founded upon a poor theory, are justified by experience'. However, as Gérard Bouchard has shown in his study of Sennely-en-Sologne, one of the masterpieces of local history, social and cultural factors played a part. In fact the régime was undergoing constant modification to cope with changing landowning patterns and the reduction of common lands.

> A decisive phenomenon was the simultaneous activity of the nobility and the bourgeoisie of the towns who were, at the beginning of the seventeenth century, undertaking the conquest of the lands of Sologne ... Neither the cultivation of the land, the raising of livestock, nor the fishing of ponds and lakes brought in enough for the locals to make a profit ... This is not to suggest that their economic activity as a whole produced no profit; only that the inhabitants were deprived of it as a result of a social organization which directed the excess yield towards the towns of Orléans, Sully, Gien or even Paris, to the advantage of a class of non-producers: nobles and bourgeois, magistrates or merchants, royal officials or *rentiers*. (Bouchard, pp. 202–6)

In this situation, where visible peasant wealth was taxed by the state, there was no incentive for an agricultural revolution. In such a system the great mass of peasants lived on a subsistence level, more prosperous in the good years and fighting for survival if there was a succession of bad ones. A rainy summer or a bad hailstorm could reduce a harvest to very little.

The consequence was greater peasant indebtedness; indeed, money or seed advanced to a peasant by the better off, the rural merchant, the *coq du village*, the seigneur or landowner, would be charged at interest and the rate was often exorbitant, for the peasants were illiterate and

21

often innumerate. Eventually, a piece of land would have to be relinquished to pay the debt. For all these reasons the peasant holding tended to decrease in size from the sixteenth century while the population increased. The numbers of the very poor rose until perhaps one-fifth of the population was permanently indigent, while the proportion would increase in time of crisis. The demographic response to the whole situation was a rise in the age of first marriages, as young people were forced to delay marriage until they had the possibility of setting up a home, and a rise in the numbers of people who remained celibate.

Amongst this mass of the population social mobility was low and much of it was downward. Few made it to the top of the village hierarchy in any case, and further advance depended on moving to the town. There were gradations of prosperity in the village, from day-labourers through the large numbers who owned only a few acres to the richer peasants. The village community was not a monolithic social structure for it had social divisions and dominating groups. Numerous local studies have revealed that above the mass of peasants were families of *laboureurs*, wealthier peasants who owned more land themselves and were able to rent larger farms or *métairies*. The distinguishing feature of the *laboureur* was ownership of a team of horses or oxen and a plough. They numbered perhaps one in ten families, but of these many were still comparatively poor and only two or three in a village might be very well off. These men would become involved in administering the seigneurial dues or other rents, and be spokesmen for the village, and with the priest, the notary and the agent of the seigneur they were at the top of the local hierarchy. Rétif de La Bretonne has left us a close description of two of them, his father and grandfather, during the first half of the eighteenth century. *My Father's Life* is a mine of information for the historian and it gives us a vivid insight into the social relations and lifestyle of this social level. This sort of information is hard to deduce from drier documents such as inventories after death and even letters or *livres de raison*. Rétif's father was a stern patriarchal character like his father before him, and was unquestioned master of the family. His working domain was the traditional male one: the agricultural tasks, the upkeep of the animals, except the barnyard ones, and the business activities of the household. He spent his day outdoors, but when he returned in the evening he was waited upon. He was not expected, or allowed, to do anything in the home, because his wife's domain was the home and the yard and she it was who managed the serving girls and was in charge of the kitchen. This division of labour was typical of the household economy of rural families and it has continued well into the twentieth century in many areas.

At the bottom of the family hierarchy came the servants, who formed a large percentage of the population, not only in urban areas but also in the rural world. As we have seen, girls and boys from about the age of twelve would serve in a better-off family for board and lodging and a

22

small, sometimes not paid, yearly sum. Servants were unquestionably usually better off than in their own harsher milieu, but all their advantages would be forfeit if their master died or the job was otherwise lost. Motherhood was incompatible with their functions, and children often had to be abandoned. Employers often fathered illegitimate children and yet might then dismiss the maidservant out of hand. J.-P. Gutton cites the example of a twenty-five-year-old serving girl, pregnant by another farm worker, being dismissed by two employers when they discovered she was pregnant. A municipal document relates that 'Not knowing what was to become of her to have her baby, being absolutely destitute, she arrived today in the present town where she is in the greatest poverty, without any means, and even ignorant of where she will stay or in whose house she will give birth'.

As we have seen, most of the surplus wealth produced by the peasantry went to the seigneur, the landowners, the church (as both landowner and spiritual provider) and the state. The first three tended to collect their dues in kind and the produce would then be converted into cash at a favourable moment. Peasants had to bring their surplus to market in the autumn, in order to acquire money from the towns to pay their taxes and rents, but then prices were low. Those who could afford to wait, the rich, could sell when the price rose after Christmas, or even when it was high in the spring and summer. Thus, the richer townspeople not only owned a lot of the land but also profited further from the peasant's situation in the market. This helps to explain the tensions between town and country at various moments in French history, for example at the time of the Revolution.

The remaining 10–15 per cent of the population lived in the towns. The vast majority of these were small market towns catering for the locality and containing a population of between 2,000 and 10,000. They would have regular markets and some would have larger fairs at certain times of the year. The pattern of trade was from the market town to the local waterway or road then to larger towns or the sea. A rural and urban merchant class, often adventurous and intrepid in its assumption of great risks, directed the trade. This group could be self-conscious, but the more usual pattern was for mercantile money to flow into safer investments. An urban bourgeoisie grew up which gradually dissociated itself from commerce by investing in land and offices. More prestigious and less risky, these investments enabled the family to move up the social scale, perhaps as far as a place in the ranks of the nobility, after several generations.

The economy of some towns was dominated by the local market and the presence of office-holders and clerics. A town of only 5–6,000, such as Rodez or Senlis, would have several churches, a cathedral and chapter, some convents and abbeys and the local courts. Other towns were centres of manufactures. In an age when most industries were still rural, iron forging and glass making for example, the most important urban manufactures were textiles. As in Beauvais or Amiens, large towns these, the production of textiles gave employment to large numbers of artisans in small workshops. Master craftsmen organized in corporations dominated the textile industry as they did other trades. Although Colbert may have encouraged them as a means of improving quality and policing the trades, corporations were often oligarchical groups determined to prevent competition from other merchants and to keep out newcomers. As an intendant wrote in the eighteenth century:

> Anyone who comes forward in the hope of obtaining a patent of mastercraftsman is subjected to the greatest difficulties, when the masters think that, by his capacity, his skill and his knowledge, he might prejudice their interests. The objections they raise consume a part of the capital which he intended to use either for his trade or to set himself up to practice his profession; and, if he does manage to have himself admitted to a mastership, it is to him that the older masters pay particular attention in the course of their inspections: he is obliged to sustain cases brought against him out of jealousy which finally cause his entire ruin.

The workers of certain trades responded by forming groups known as *compagnonnages* to organize mutual aid and resist the employment practices of the masters. Litigation between them and masters was not infrequent.

Life in the towns was not very much better than it was in the countryside. The dwellings were as cold and unpleasant and life was lived in the street and in the tavern or *cabaret*. Existence was just as precarious. High bread prices would unleash an economic crisis as workers and peasants could no longer afford to buy anything but bread and so the production of other goods had to be cut. A textile worker of Lille recorded the effects of the major crisis of 1692:

> At the beginning of the month of September grain and flour became so expensive, to begin with it went up so much in two days ... and we didn't know where to find the money ... and the poor people could not live because the trades closed down and we had no wages to live ... Some poor people bought flour to make bread, and the bread was as if it was all rotten, red and black, and the poor folk took it to the Town Hall to show it to the gentlemen of the Council and it was a great shame to see it and many were crying and I saw it and held it in my own hands ... many were then abandoning their wives and children to the Magistrates because they could not feed them, on account of the high price of bread and of the low wages and no work ... Oh God what a cruel time. (Lottin, 1977)

The insanitary, overcrowded environment was a perfect target for epidemics. The rich would flee to their country homes until the plague had run its course. Other disasters could occur too; the passage of troops was invariably one, though marginally less so after Le Tellier's army reforms of the 1660s.

Most towns were privileged with respect to royal taxation, having at some point in their history established by purchase or agreement exemption from the tithe and other taxes. However, royal fiscality began to put ever greater pressure on them during the seventeenth and eighteenth centuries. Forced loans were levied on municipal finances, useless municipal offices were created and their purchase imposed upon the towns, and indirect taxes were levied on the entry and exit of goods. The oligarchically controlled municipalities usually managed to throw the burden of these taxes on to the poorer classes by creating urban sales taxes, especially on drinks, to replenish the municipal coffers. 'It can be said of the municipal officers that the greatest of public matters concerns them less than the smallest of private interests.' The result was a proliferation of bars in the faubourgs.

In spite of the intendants' efforts to control town finances, municipal indebtedness went on increasing until the Revolution, not because of incompetence but because of the demands of the state. In 1718, after the expedients of the War of the Spanish Succession, Nantes had debts of 346,517 *livres*. In 1782 Rennes had a revenue of 222,360 *livres* 5 *sous* and 3 *deniers*, and of this paid 67,028*l* 15*s* 9*d* to the state. In 1778 the intendant of Brittany wrote that 'The towns of this province are very heavily endebted. The obligations and ordinary expenditures consume almost their entire revenue, such that it is impossible for them to provide for the repair and maintenance of the public works.'

At the top of the social scale was the order of nobility. Originally a military order, with its origins in the landowning elite of the Dark Ages and the ruling military families of the era of Charlemagne and his successors, the nobility was exempt from personal direct taxation on the grounds that it paid its tax in blood. The feudal system had ensured a noble large landholdings, cultivated by serfs or free peasants owing dues to their lord, in order that he and his retainers might form a fighting force in the service of the king. Serfdom had virtually disappeared by the sixteenth century but the landholdings, the seigneurial system and the dues remained. Military prowess, honour and virtue were at the roots of the aristocratic ethic, although from the late sixteenth century this was increasingly influenced by notions of urbane or courtly manners and nobles were more receptive to the new educational pattern based on Renaissance humanism. Here it may be noted that Castiglione's *The Book of the Courtier* was vastly influential and books of etiquette were an important literary genre for all classes of society in the ancien régime. This nobility of the sword was neither an entirely rural group nor a fully urban one, for it was customary to have a château or manor in the seigneurie, with the reserve of land cultivated directly for profit, and by the seventeenth century often a grand residence in town built in the Renaissance or classical style. It need hardly be said that these *hôtels* and those built by affluent merchants in the big sea-ports remain a feature of the architecture of many provincial towns today, while in Paris the Marais contains many restored aristocratic dwellings. As ever in France, there is a regional difference in that in the Midi, with its urban traditions, the nobility tended to live in the towns, whereas in the north and west of France they lived more in the country, even into the eighteenth century.

Nobility was transmissible through the male line in France, so at first sight the nobility would appear to have been a military caste, and for a long time this is how it conceived of itself. However, to accept this would be to ignore the very significant developments taking place during the sixteenth century. There had always been a certain amount of upward mobility by the bourgeoisie, but that century was marked by significant usurpation of nobility by former members of the landed bourgeoisie. They first lived in noble style then, with the prestige acquired from this, simply became accepted as such in the area and were finally integrated by marriage into the local nobility. The other group joining the nobility in large numbers was the elite of the venal office-holders whose posts conferred life nobility upon the incumbent and the rank of hereditary noble upon the family after it had held such an office for, usually, three generations. Towards the end of the ancien régime, Necker calculated that there were about 4,000 ennobling offices in France. This administrative nobility, the nobility of the robe (after the long or short black robe worn by officers of justice) was at first much resented by the sword nobility. The Estates General of 1614 witnessed particularly vociferous denunciations of venality of office, and as late as the eighteenth century a snobbish duke of recent creation, Saint-Simon, could even denounce this 'vile bourgeoisie'.

However, too much has been made of the distinction, for recent local studies of the early-seventeenth-century nobility have revealed that the new groups were rapidly assimilated. Even the noble ethic changed under the impact of a robe ideological offensive and it came to include the Renaissance idea of virtue as an honourable trait identifiable from high robe activities. The salon world of the seventeenth century did much to achieve this ethical union, while extensive intermarriage knitted the groups together until all that remained of the division was the choice of two careers – and this certainly by the mid seventeenth century everywhere except in some corners of the court and amongst the families of the most ancient higher nobility. Whatever its social origins, and we shall return to this later, the nobility was the most powerful group in society by virtue of its social rank, its landed wealth, its military power, and its role in government. Even the upper reaches of the ecclesiastical hierarchy were almost exclusively filled by aristocrats: from the early sixteenth century to the Revolution around 85–90 per cent of the episcopate was

26

recruited from noble families. This was partly because the crown found it useful to exploit the enormous revenues of the church in order to placate and sustain powerful aristocratic houses.

Unfortunately, it is impossible to arrive at an accurate and verifiable estimate of the size of the nobility in France. For 1789 estimates vary from 200,000 individuals to 400,000, and these figures certainly represent an increase of the numbers since the sixteenth century, for the eighteenth century saw an expansion of the aristocracy. Research in some provinces has shown that over the centuries the noble proportion of the population remained at a fairly constant 1–1.5 per cent. On the other hand, in the pre-revolutionary period the nobility owned about 20 per cent of the land. Once again, it need hardly be said that there were regional variations: in the north, Picardy, Artois, the west and Burgundy it was a particularly high proportion, whereas in the centre, the south, and the south-east it was lower. Even using tax rolls and the sales of noble land during the Revolution it has been impossible to calculate accurately the extent of the ownership. In Brie it was 35 per cent, in Burgundy 40 per cent, in Auvergne 11 per cent, around Montpellier 15 per cent, whereas it was 40 per cent around Toulouse.

Within this group differences of wealth could be enormous. The provincial nobility was, in spite of complaints about its poverty to the king, almost always the richest group in the area even if a few of its members were relatively poor. But provincial families could rarely compete in terms of wealth with the grand houses drawing revenue from extensive properties in several provinces, court offices and pensions, governorships and ecclesiastical sinecures. Most dukes were, quite simply, vastly wealthy, and by their presence at court were well able to defend their family interests. Indeed, their extravagant life-styles required huge expenditure and therefore demanded a constant pressure at court to replenish finances, as Robert Forster has shown in his case study of *The House of Saulx-Tavannes*. Differences of wealth were obviously of some importance in the nobility, but what counted most was the antiquity of the lineage and its degree of nobility. Here two concepts are important: misalliance and *dérogeance*. The latter was the loss of noble status for engaging in any non-noble activity, such as retail trade, although wholesale trade was allowed, and fear of it conditioned noble commercial strategies. Misalliance was a term to describe the joining by marriage of a noble and rich bourgeois family. Important as these concepts were to nobles, we should remember that the words would not have existed had they not been useful to describe something which was actually practised!

No analysis of society, and especially of the early modern French aristocracy, would be complete without a discussion of the patterns of social mobility. An understanding of social mobility is vital to enable us to take a position in the historical controversies over the nature of the nobility, the bourgeoisie and the structure of society itself. Social mobility reveals not only the internal workings of society but also social values and aspirations. In theory, it would be possible to examine all the social levels in a town, together with the marriages within and between social groups, and arrive at precise conclusions. Unfortunately, the records do not permit the identification of all individuals within their classes, and complete sets of records are rare in any case – to which problems must be added the fact that the essential quantitative methods involving the use of computers have become available only recently. Historians therefore have to rely upon local studies, case histories of individual families and the more easily compiled information on the nobility at the pinnacle of society.

Patterns of social mobility near the bottom of the social scale are difficult to discern, and certainly any significant advance took place over several generations. Probably the *coq du village* would acquire more land and more rented farms, whilst becoming the agent for a seigneur and perhaps acting as a local judge, like Edmé Rétif de la Bretonne. His son would be given a better education (literacy was essential for mobility) and might continue to rise slowly until he became a substantial property-owner in the locality, eventually living off his investments. More probable was the use of education and connections through the seigneur to acquire some legal or fiscal office in the town or with an aristocratic household as a more important agent. Accumulated wealth would be invested in land and in more impressive and lucrative offices. The family would become a member of the urban bourgeoisie and acquire a certain social esteem, denoted by the adoption of minor titles associated with fiefs. 'Noble homme' or 'honneste homme' would qualify his name in local records. If a merchant already had wealth, he would invest it in the safe returns from land rather than the risky business of trade, and would enter the course at a later stage, perhaps as a minor office-holder. Such was the probable route to a stage about which historians know a great deal more, the transition from the wealthy bourgeoisie to the new nobility.

A member of the bourgeoisie, even if he himself was content with his status, would hope for advancement for his family through his sons and daughters. Jean Maillefer, a wholesale cloth merchant and bourgeois of Reims, thought like this in the 1670s. 'For a long time I was tormented by temptations about my dislikes; at the present time I am tempted by vanity for the advancement of my children, believing that I have as much wealth as those I see display their dignity by the external trappings of wealth and that encourages me. . .' (Durand, p. 52). Far from wishing acceptance in the upper reaches of Rémois society as a bourgeois he, like almost all members of the bourgeoisie until 1789, was prepared to ascend by the established paths which led to nobility. The first stage involved a particularly French concept, that of *rentier*, someone who lives off his investments. Several types of *rente* were available: interest on loans to the province, the municipality or the king, in that order of preference; life annuities; landed rents and seigneurial dues; the income from offices. Several of these would frequently be combined at one time, the important thing was to be seen not to work and thus to begin to live nobly. In order for him to rise further the institution of venality of office was the most vital channel. Eventually, an ennobling office would be acquired, and after perhaps four or five generations a family might have risen from the level of a merchant or seigneurial agent to that of first generation noble, an *anobli*. The family had almost arrived, but not quite. It remained to consolidate the new social situation by intermarriage with other members of the nobility. Marriage was a second vital factor in social mobility, not usually as an upward path in itself, for marriages between unequal partners were rare, but as a combination of two equal fortunes. Thus bakers married bakers' daughters, masters-to-be married the daughters of other master craftsmen, bourgeois married bourgeoises and so on, to the level of duke and peer. A good marriage with dowry would increase the capital available to a family for its ascension. In the final assessment, it was money that counted, whatever the social myths at the time may lead us to believe.

Of all the social and professional groups in the ancien régime, the financier was the most mobile – upward, and often downward, as he was in a risky business. Corruption was an entirely relative concept in that age, and there were vast profits to be made from handling the finances of the state. Fiscal offices were a question of private enterprise and a certain amount of money, often quite a large sum, was quite legitimately retained by the agent. Financial agents and tax collectors centralizing large sums were naturally also bankers lending the state money at interest and pocketing the profits – and this was also quite legitimate. Or they might be members of that hated and despised group, the *traitants* or *partisans* as they were called, men responsible for collecting taxes on monopolies they had purchased from, and often suggested to, the crown, or inventing and selling more offices. Supplying the army was another way of making huge fortunes, as in the case of the famous Pâris brothers in the first half of the eighteenth century. But the figure of the financier *par excellence* is that of the Farmer General, one of a group of forty who farmed the indirect taxes throughout much of France from the seventeenth century. Daughters of rich financiers could find a ready match with an old but penurious noble family, and the enormous wealth of many of the Farmers General meant that they were accepted by high society in the eighteenth century without acquiring nobility, by virtue of their display, culture and artistic patronage.

Mobility was slow, individual mobility practically nil, but over several generations it was significant, especially for the composition of the nobility, and money was essential. However, towards the upper reaches of society, competition became keen for offices and letters of nobility from the king. A final factor was equally essential – patronage. Mousnier expressed this neatly in the conclusion to a symposium on social mobility: 'At each stage of ascension, favour is indispensable, the favour of a *grand seigneur*, of a *grand officier*, then of a member of the governing group: chancellor, surintendant, prince of the blood, another prince, a minister.

Favour is indispensable in order to get through the bottlenecks which occur at various stages, to get to the highest ranks in society – it is just as necessary as a multiplicity of occupations' (*XVIIe siècle*, 1979).

Influenced as we are today by notions culled from sociology and political science, we recognize the importance of social mobility for social stability. Frustration at being blocked at a less-prestigious rank in society than one's aspirations would have it can lead to conflict and violence. Indeed, as we have seen, this is an explanation for the bourgeois revolution.

Social mobility was so slow and the sense of historical time so undeveloped that to most men of the ancien régime society appeared immutably set in a pre-ordained tripartite order. The division into three orders or estates has Indo-European origins and was accepted as axiomatic from the eleventh century, according to G. Duby's brilliant study *Feudal Society Imagined*. The first order was the *oratores*, those who prayed; the second the *bellatores*, those who fought; and the third the *laboratores* whose destiny it was to work to support the other two. This schema formed a part of the divinely created hierarchy and was an earthly imitation of the society of angels. It was so deeply embedded in the medieval and early modern mind that it had become enshrined in the legal ordering of society, with different courts, laws and penalties for each estate. By the seventeenth century it was clear to Loyseau, whose description of society, the *Book of Orders* (1606), was much republished throughout the century, that the three orders included only the elite of society and did not extend to the whole nation. Like Seyssel a century earlier, he divided society into four parts. The fourth part was the vile populace, the rabble, from whom no good could come, and this part was vile because it lived by manual labour. In the late Middle Ages politics and the development of representative institutions had brought the reality of four orders to light but in none of the Estates General, including the final meeting of 1789, was the peasant or the unorganized town labourer represented in terms of deputies. The notion that manual labour was vile ensured that no practical modification to the tripartite conception was justified. However, it is important to recognize that the idea of estates extended beyond the orders and was a concept that was fundamental to social organization. The word 'estate' had a wide range of meaning, for it also meant profession, rank and dignity, and thus it was the basis for the organization of groups into corporations.

Olivier-Martin, Coornaert and, more recently, W. H. Sewell, working on the corporate idiom, have done much to elucidate the importance of corporate bodies in a society of orders. Corporate society began at the level of those who were thought to apply some art or intelligence to their manual labour, namely at the level of the wide variety of urban trades. Such trades (*arts et métiers*) were often possessors of royal or local statutes recognizing them as a legal person or community with rules and regulations, rights and privileges, and a religious brotherhood. Masters of the trades controlled such corporations and they were responsible for their own *police*. Higher up the social scale came the liberal professions and then the royal office-holders, most of whom were also organized in a corps (the word 'corporation' was usually only applied to the less-prestigious corporate bodies). The intendants were all recruited from the corps of masters of requests; the financial officials in the *élections* were in a syndicate of the *élus*; and the universities had a corporate existence in a way that was not fundamentally different from the order of the clergy or the several parlements of France. In the Middle Ages and the sixteenth century not all professions had corporate bodies, but because the crown found the system convenient both administratively and financially it encouraged the corporate régime to the extent that it became the normal form by the late seventeenth century. Although the ideal was one of order and hierarchy, as so often during the ancien régime, the reality was very different. Conflicts between corporations were constant, and if such bodies gave the masters security they also served to oppress the apprentices and journeymen.

This legal division of society into corporations and orders is entirely accepted by historians. What is still a matter for dispute is whether or not the legal conception, powerful influence on men's minds though it was, actually implies that society was not a society of classes. According to the class view, the most important divisions for the purposes of historical understanding and for contemporary motivations were economic ones which led to solidarities within classes or groups of similar economic standing: class struggle was therefore a reality. At present, most historians would tend to say that it was not, at least until the late eighteenth century. Nevertheless, the issue has provoked much debate and research. The dispute has focused principally upon two periods: the middle decades of the seventeenth century and the decades preceding the Revolution

The former was an era of endemic peasant revolts which also saw the parlementaire and princely Fronde. In 1948 the Soviet historian Porsnev published a book on *Popular Uprisings in France from 1623 to 1648*. He maintained that the neglected topic of revolts provided considerable evidence of class fronts formed by the propertied elite, including the bourgeoisie, against the popular classes. He argued that the state itself was an aristocratic state, which served the nobility and sections of the bourgeoisie even though the rising taxes did become a source of discontent within this elite. The revolts were desperate uprisings against seigneurial exploitation in a world whose economy remained essentially feudal, in the Marxist sense of a medieval land-based economy. According to Porsnev, the failure of the bourgeoisie to effect a revolution during the Fronde can only be explained by its still feudal conceptions and role. The bourgeoisie had been feudalized by the state instead of developing its capitalist role and its revolutionary future lay in the eighteenth century.

Mousnier objected to this analysis on several counts. First, he claimed, on a good documentary basis, that popular revolts were not spontaneous and anti-feudal but were anti-fiscal, and more often than not provoked by the active or passive resistance to royal taxation by the seigneurs, who were often also magistrates. This cooperation between seigneur and peasant was a feature of society which disproves the existence of class fronts. Instead, Mousnier substituted the idea of vertical links between seigneur and peasant, patron and client. Second, he pointed to the spread of a money economy and capitalist relations in the countryside to prove that the economy was no longer feudal in the sense of the manorial economy of the high Middle Ages. Therefore, the seigneurial system of the seventeenth century was very different from the medieval system. Third, the state was not an instrument of the propertied feudal class, but was a force in its own right which rose above the nobility and the bourgeoisie. Their struggles against this development mark a stage in the history of the state. 'To see the absolutist monarchical state as the agent of an economically dominant class, whose interests it assured through the oppression of other classes, seems to me to be an error.' The debate gave a great impetus to research, which at first did much to confirm and extend Mousnier's conclusions. Mousnier himself later developed the idea that society was one of orders and estates, not of classes, and that solidarities were those of family, community and fidelity.

Twenty years later it is possible to suggest that the early interpretations of popular revolts undervalued the language of the crowd. Research on popular mentalities and ritualistic behaviour is proving that what is portrayed, in the sources written by the elite, as senseless, angry, popular outbursts actually possessed a moral rationale that escaped the observers who no longer shared the same values. This is especially true of the *taxations populaires* exercised in times of high prices, when the populace would force the sale of grain or bread at a 'just price' in the market. There is also a certain amount of evidence that the peasantry thoroughly disliked the seigneurial system in its early modern form, because the seigneur was rarely an advocate of the peasant and was more often an oppressor. Of course, from the Sire de Gouberville in the sixteenth century to the Marquis de Ferrières in 1789 there were seigneurs who felt a duty towards their peasants. Society could hardly have functioned had relations been perpetually antagonistic, but one suspects that the more usual advocate of the peasant was not the lord but the prosperous villager, such as Rétif de la Bretonne's father. The *cahiers* of 1789, some earlier revolts and the constant attempts at the evasion of rights and dues all reveal widespread anti-seigneurial feelings. In Sennely-en-Sologne a prior described the peasant attitude in 1700: 'They are all sworn enemies of their masters, of their superiors; they eternally ponder the means to harm them either by cheating them, or by slandering them, or by revealing the confidences entrusted to them. They rail at any superiority. In their own company they maintain no respect for persons of quality of all conditions ... In the presence of their masters they appear humble and submissive: but when their backs are turned they take their revenge in a hundred different ways. They tear them to pieces with the blackest impostures, mock them, imitate them and, what is worse, cleverly cheat them at the first opportunity.' Mitigating the effects of this sentiment and discouraging open revolt was a profound respect for tradition and the existing hierarchy. However, several popular revolts began, directed against fiscal innovations and, as in Aix-en-Provence in 1630, subsequently turned against all those rich enough to profit from the organization of the new taxes. It must therefore be emphasized that in certain situations the dividing line between the possessors of substantial property and the rest was a fundamental cleavage. On each side of the line there was an awareness of the situation, and ultimately the propertied feared the disorderly populace more than they did the power of the crown. Whether or not the division represents a class consciousness is hardly important except for Marxist theorists.

The reader will have noticed the extent to which Mousnier's arguments still fitted in with the orthodox view, and many wonder if the research has therefore confirmed it. Before resolving this question other factors should be considered. Ancien régime society was far more complex than participants in the debate seemed to admit. Although Porsnev and Mousnier were both consummate masters of seventeenth-century history, each developed a thesis which, when generalized, does not do full justice to the reality. Part of the problem lies in the fact that insufficient research has been carried out on the social vocabulary and on socio-economic groups, and that therefore historical categories are unclear.

One aspect of this complexity is well illustrated by the conclusions that may be drawn from a wealth of new material on the early modern nobility. The orthodox view of a crisis of the nobility in the late sixteenth century and its partial replacement by a new bourgeoisie had never been systematically proved. Recent studies of the fortunes of specific aristocratic houses and of the composition of the nobility in Normandy have revealed that the old nobility survived the period of price inflation very well, and that the numbers of poor nobles did not increase. Falls in seigneurial dues were usually compensated for by rises in rents and profits from the directly farmed estate, and there was no extensive sale of fiefs and manors to the bourgeoisie (Wood, 1980). Numerous studies have proved the continued dominance of the nobility in the eighteenth century, in Brittany, Provence, Burgundy, Toulouse and the Bordelais. It has also been shown that the old nobility was by no means a closed caste. It can only be defined as comprising families that had been noble for four generations or more, rather than those that could trace their nobility back to, say, the fourteenth century. The rate of extinction of noble families was high because the house required a male heir, who was not always forthcoming, and wars took a heavy toll of aristocratic sons. In the Forez only 5 out of 215 families survived or remained in the area from the thirteenth century to 1789 and yet the percentage of noble families in the population remained constant. The ancien régime nobility was actually a group to which access was far easier than was once thought. This being so, it is unnecessary to postulate a crisis to explain a certain amount of upward and downward mobility. By 1789 probably nearly one-half of the nobility was more recent than the mid sevententh century. As has been shown, patterns of mobility and local studies reveal that wealth was one of its characteristics. Thus, the nobility was a group which thought of itself as an exclusive order but which was actually largely an economic group able to afford to live nobly. For this reason it thrived throughout the period and showed no signs of decline in the eighteenth century. By then the richest court nobles were owners, either directly or through front-men, of ironworks, ships and mineral resources, which they were exploiting in a thoroughly capitalist way, just as they did their seigneurial dues and landed estates. Amongst others, Forster's studies of *The Nobility of Toulouse* and *The House of Saulx-Tavannes* provide proof of this.

If the nobility could sometimes look very capitalist, the bourgeoisie has come to seem far less so than it once appeared. There is a problem of terminology, because the ancien régime notion of bourgeois did not necessarily or usually imply capitalism, as it did to Marx in the nineteenth century. The word 'bourgeoisie' had a wide variety of meanings, from rich peasant to master of a shop or member of the urban elite. Juridically, a bourgeois was a man of status and privilege living in a town, owning landed estates and living rather like a noble. Alfred Cobban has shown that the men of 1789 were of this type, lawyers and office-holders, not capitalists. According to Marcel Reinhard the bourgeoisie was in the process of merging with the nobility to form a class of notables who eventually came to rule France in the nineteenth century. An American historian, G.V. Taylor (1967), has shown that it is a mistake to equate the bourgeoisie with modern capitalist wealth, because there was very little such wealth in the ancien régime. Bourgeois aspirations remained fixed on status and the chief result of the expansion of their numbers produced by the commercial gains of the eighteenth century was an increased demand for office and noble titles. In the light of these conclusions it is hard to identify an increasingly revolutionary bourgeoisie. The traditional historical categories seem to have proved inadequate to explain events and the new analyses paint a very different picture for which orders and classes are too simple a notion. From the bottom of rural society to the top of the urban hierarchy, wealth, family and function seem to have together generated the social groups of the ancien régime.

No modern survey of the regime should fail to take account of the long-term movement in the economy and the developments in trade. The early modern economy, as measured by statistics of prices, which are unfortunately not decisive indicators, falls into three phases. From about 1480 to 1640 there was expansion and a price rise. There followed a century-long depression until the 1730s, when there was a new upturn. These long phases were cut by periodic intercycles, such as the downturn from 1778 into the 1790s. In his classic study of Languedoc, Le Roy Ladurie has portrayed the human response in the short term to these changes in the economic climate over a much longer period. There can be no doubt that the development of such quantitative and interdisciplinary history has made a contribution of great importance for the understanding of this era. Such scholars as Simiand, Labrousse, Meuvret, Chaunu and Goubert have provided the statistical data with which to interpret the evolution of an economic system over several centuries.

Although the manufacture of textiles was an important industry, it must not be imagined that manufactures were either concentrated in factories or able to rival agriculture in importance. Production was overwhelmingly artisanal and even in the eighteenth century only a few factories, or royal manufactures, existed, such as the Gobelins tapestry works. There was a sense of dignity attached to labour which was only to disappear during the industrial revolution of the nineteenth century. In comparison to the total agricultural production, foreign trade was low. Around 1700 foreign trade reached perhaps 215 million *livres* as against roughly 1300 million *livres* in agriculture. On the eve of the Revolution the figures had increased to 1100 million and 2600 million respectively, changing the ratio to 2:5. Clearly, there was increased circulation in the economy and the development of new wealth, especially in the sea-ports, such as La Rochelle, Bordeaux and Nantes, whose architecture bears witness to this expansion. The opening up of the Baltic and transatlantic trade had much to do with this, as the basis of the European economy shifted during the seventeenth century away from the Mediterranean towards the New World and the north. These developments affected the internal economy of France and also had the effect of widening the mental horizons of the educated.

2 The Mind of the Ancien Régime

A generation ago few general books gave much space to the way contemporaries viewed the world during the ancien régime. Today a large volume would hardly suffice to cover adequately the newly researched material! French historians have been painstakingly at work to explore the patterns of belief and the world view, or *mentalité*, of the mass of the population, not forgetting the solidarities and sociability networks created by the routines of everyday life in small, isolated communities. Much of the evidence for the common people comes either directly from the literate classes or was mediated by them. These classes were steadily moving away from the popular culture during our period, indeed they were often busy repressing popular practices, and their evidence sheds as much light upon its own authors as upon their subjects. For this reason the fears, prejudices and beliefs of the upper classes also stand revealed, open to the prying eye of the historian. Their beliefs were often a far cry from the world of humanism and enlightenment so often associated with them. This briefest of introductions will explore the many facets of the new history and explain the context in which the early modern state operated.

Before examining the *mentalité* of Frenchmen during the ancien régime we should consider the social conceptions that gave society its very structure. Embodied in the form of institutions and referred to in innumerable texts, these notions were three: hierarchy, corporatism and privilege. None of these principles is specific to the ancien régime, for all of them date back into the medieval period, and their precise origins are indeterminable. Even now the medieval conception of a great chain of being was still a powerful notion. The chain ran from the angels down to the lowest of inanimate objects, passing through human society in all its fine gradations of rank, in a divinely ordained and natural hierarchy. Everyone had his place, which ought to be accepted without discontent, and ambitious attempts to change places in the social order were therefore condemned. Appearance was important and it was considered appropriate to display the difference in one's social position by external marks such as dress or accoutrements: for example, the noble should never be separated from his sword. Display and ostentation were therefore essential to the higher social ranks and nobles could find that keeping up their dignity by appearance was a costly affair. But everybody, even the peasantry, was aware of the proper hierarchy, for it was paraded in the ceremonial order of processions which were such a feature of early modern life. Many engravings exist of *entrées* and processions, and much can be learned about the gradations in the social order from studying them. As late as the mid eighteenth century a bourgeois of Montpellier chose to describe town society in the order in which groups participated in processions, and he reiterated age-old complaints that unworthy persons were imitating the dress of their social superiors (Darnton, 1984).

As we have already seen in the previous chapter, corporations were as fundamental to the structure of the régime as was hierarchy itself. Corporatism was embodied in all the institutions of the period, and the corporation was the framework in which the individual existed and acquired honour, dignity and identity. No procession had a place for an individual, only for a member of a legally constituted body, for the individual had no station as such. By the seventeenth century almost every professional group had formed itself into a corporation, with its patron saint, ceremonial, regulations and its place in the hierarchy. This was as true of tailors as it was of judicial officers wielding authority on behalf of the king.

Every corporation or order had its collection of rights or privileges. The word 'privilege' came to have a pejorative meaning at the time of the Revolution, but the notion was fundamental to the ancien régime. It meant a right or distinction, useful or honorific, enjoyed by certain members of society and guaranteed in law. In fact, privilege pertained more to groups and institutions than to individuals, exceptions to this rule being favoured persons at court and some economic monopolies. The first two orders in society were privileged, numerous courts of justice had privileges of jurisdiction, whole provinces were privileged in that they were exempt from, say, the salt tax, or direct taxation by royal agents, and they also tended to have their own legal codes, and the *bonnes villes* were privileged towns because they had acquired fiscal exemptions. Thus, a peasant or town labourer could be privileged in relation to someone in another village or town, and the concept may be seen to have permeated society at all levels. A full description of the privileges of even one town would fill a small volume, so more than these brief indications is clearly out of the question here. No doubt the notion itself stems from the medieval vision of the basic inequality of man and the justice of distinctions, but it was encouraged by the monarchy, which tended to sell privileges when short of cash. In many cases *privilège* is synonymous with *liberté*, which meant not at all our own abstract conception of freedom enjoyed by everyone and bound up with natural rights, but a concrete right belonging to a group. In political theory the existence of liberties and privileges ensured that France did not degenerate into a tyranny or despotism.

The sense of insecurity and the precariousness of this earthly existence led to an obsession with order, the final keyword of the era. In many literary and artistic works we find the opposition of disorder/order, just as we do high/low. There were fears of cosmic disorders, popular disorders and the dissolution of the hierarchical, corporate, privileged society. Jean Bodin in the late sixteenth century expressed the need for order in terms that would have been accepted well into the eighteenth century (Six Books, pp. 386–7):

> For if it is true that in all things we desire and seek after a convenient and decent order, and consider nothing to be more ugly or dirty to look upon than confusion and disorder: then how much more is it to be sought for in a Commonweale, so to place citizens or subjects in such apt and comely order so that the first may be joined with the last and they in the middle with both; and so all with all in a most true knot and bond among themselves together with the Commonweale? For it is a most ancient and received opinion of the wise, Almighty God himself, the great and supreme workmaster and creator of this great and wonderful Fabrick of all things in the creating thereof to have performed nothing either greater or better than that He ... so settled everything in its due place and order. Neither can there be anything fairer to behold, more delightful to the mind or more useful than is order itself. But they who go about so as to make all subjects and citizens equal one to another in dignity order and place, so that there shall be nothing in a Commonweale first, or in the middle but will have all degrees so mingled and confounded without respect to sex, age or condition; they seem to me to act as do those who thrust barley, wheat, rice and millet and all other kinds of grain together into one heap; whereby they lose the use both of every kind of grain in particular, and also of the whole heap together.
>
> For the above reasons there was never any lawgiver so unskillful but that he thought there ought to be some division ordering or sorting of the citizens or subjects in a city or Commonweale. Here by ordering or sorting the citizens or subjects, my meaning is that there should be a part of the citizens divided from the rest in condition, state or sex: in sex as women from men; in state as free borne men from them which are but of manumised serfs.

In the preservation of order all had a part to play, but the monarch had a special importance as the defender of the social hierarchy. He stood for order and his duty it was to arbitrate disputes and repress disorders in the commonwealth, as a father did in the family. Thus, the state was necessary and the monarch was at the pinnacle of a social hierarchy of which he formed the guarantor. The result was that ancien régime society without a monarch was almost literally unthinkable, in the same way that in the sixteenth century, as L. Febvre has shown, real atheism was beyond the bounds of normal patterns of thought.

As we have seen, for the mass of the population everyday life took place in the context of the rural parish. Solidarities therefore existed upon a number of levels and these links both conditioned the way people thought and acted and were a product of pre-existing attitudes. Everybody knew each other, attended the same parish church, worked together at harvest time, shared the common lands, contributed to the collective tax levied on the parish or seigneurie, and participated in the same events in the festive calendar. The culture of the people was a local culture, the mental horizon extending to the *pays* or at most the region but certainly not taking in such concepts as the nation or the state. The family was, of course, the principal point of reference and it was a strictly hierarchical institution (in law as in practice) dominated by patriarchal authority. Other focal points for sociability were youth groups, to which young males would belong, and religious brotherhoods, usually the penitents, which became popular from the fifteenth century. Both of these groupings had the advantage of being a chosen forum for the individual, unlike the family. The youth groups, organized into mock abbeys, or *reinages*, presided over by an elected abbot or king, would play a prominent role in festivities, were associated with courting rituals and to some extent were the guardians of village morality.

Solidarities played a vital psychological role, enabling the individual to cope with the harsh economic conditions and face up to the insecurities that threatened him from all quarters. Disease and death were everywhere, deeply marking the psychology of the era. Fear and insecurity were the experience of everyone: fear of the dark, of solitude, of unknown places, of death, of evil spells, of the devil's work, of marauders and beggars in this world, and of purgatory in the next. Who could feel secure when the vital harvests were subject to the ravages of storms, and plagues were still endemic? For most, life was a brutish existence involving little dignity and much suffering – not the happy existence portrayed in Le Nain's paintings. Living so close to the breadline, people were callous, fatalistic and yet highly strung, their emotions were volatile and, on the evidence of literary texts, tears flowed more easily than in our culture today. According to Mandrou (1961), even the hierarchy of the senses was different, more emphasis being put upon hearing and touch than upon seeing, for this was not yet a literate age. Few were members of the 'Gutenberg galaxy' in which printing has reordered the presentation of information, altered the mental landscape and the patterns of thought. But let us beware of concluding, as did so many contemporaries and even historians, that the peasantry was brutalized and irrational to the extent that it was devoid of moral values. On the contrary, recent studies of demography, popular revolts, legal cases and religious practices reveal a society with a high degree of sexual morality and a sense of traditional social justice, a 'moral economy', to borrow the phrase from E.P. Thompson (1971). These works reveal a set of values relating to justice, the family, honour and the community which have long been overlooked, especially in studies of popular protest, for which the archives of the disdainful repressors have been used. For example, *taxations populaires* involved the forced selling of over-priced bread in the market-place at a 'just' price. The legal records examined by Castan (1974) reveal powerful notions of respectability in village relations. Many elements in popular culture provide evidence of the strong morality required of people in village life, the adherence to a code of values which served to protect the community and its traditions. One such occasion was the *charivari*, organized by the local youth as a punishment for transgressing the mores of the community, especially in cases of remarriage when a young woman married an older widower, depriving a youth of a potential bride. Here the rough music is described by Thomas Platter, a sixteenth-century medical student in Montpellier.

> I must say a word about charivari. This is a term that comes from the Greek and means a broken head. When, in the neighbourhood, a young man marries an old widow, or a young girl marries an aged widower, they are treated to charivari. All the young people assemble, one bringing a cauldron, another a stove or a drum, a third a fife or a salt-box with the spoon, or a trumpet, etc. The band gather in front of the couple's house and at midnight begin a concert, howling, blowing and banging with all their might. No-one in that quarter gets any sleep. Sometimes they fill the street with evil odours that make everyone gasp for breath. And this row goes on every night, for two hours or more, until the couple buy their peace by payment of a certain sum. Frequently there are brawls. (Platter, p. 122)

Such practices were a part of a rich and varied popular culture which is too vast a subject for a detailed assessment here. By studying the themes and devices in folk tales collected in the nineteenth century, or written down in the first cheap paperbacks from the mid seventeenth century (the *Bibliothèque bleue*), historians have explored some of the popular beliefs. Folk tales are full of superstition and magic, with cunning peasants outwitting or ridiculing evil lords, bandits, priests or Jews. It is a Rabelaisian world full of laughter and mockery, where traditional values are inverted and which draws heavily upon the medieval heritage of chivalry, Christianized paganisms and an apparently European stock of folk-tale types. Popular culture, and the tales in particular, was never taught formally – there were no village schools before the eighteenth century. Culture was spontaneous, drawing upon everyday life, and traditions were communicated orally. If there was a special occasion when culture was communicated, it was at the wake, or *veillée*, when in the evening women would gather to sew and the men would chat and tell tales. Only one description of this widespread practice survives – that of Noël du Fail (1928, ch. 5):

Robin Chevet was a very good fellow, upon my word, as he himself declared, and in the whole neighbourhood it was he who ploughed the best furrow. He invented, bless him, a thousand fine sayings about agriculture, which he would impart to many in good faith and without meaning any offence. Often, after supper, his belly stretched tight like a drum, bursting full, his back to the fire, he would chat, while cutting hemp neatly or repairing his boots after the latest fashion (for every respectable gentleman should follow the fashion), singing very tunefully, as he fittingly could do, some new song; from the other side of the room, his wife Joanne, sewing away, would take up the refrain likewise. The other members of the household would each be working at their task; some repairing the straps on their flail, others making teeth for rakes, or charring withers to fasten the axle of the cart, which had been broken by too high a ridge; or making a whip handle from medlar tree. And in this way, busy with different chores, the good man Robin, after having imposed silence, would begin to tell a pleasant tale about the time when animals could speak (not two hours ago): about how the fox stole the fish from the fishmonger, and how he had the wolf beaten by the washerwomen, when he was teaching him to fish; how the dog and the cat roamed far afield; or about the crow who lost the cheese when he opened his beak to sing; about Mélusine; about the werewolf; the tale of Peau-d'âne, the princess who wore a donkey's skin and married a prince; of the fairies and how he would often speak familiarly with them. . .

Perhaps the supreme expression of popular culture was carnival. Festivities centred upon harvest time, Christmas, Shrovetide, during May and on Midsummer's Eve, although innumerable other dates figured in the local calendar according to the patron-saints' days of brotherhoods, guilds and communities. Carnival was a time of relief from dispiriting conditions and an oppressive world order. It was a time of release and, significantly, of an inversion of normal values. High became low, the child and the fool reigned and constraints seemed to be cast aside. It was an orgy of gluttony, dancing, sexual symbolism (bears and sausages in particular) and ritualized licence. Historians and anthropologists have speculated much upon the deeper significance of this world-turned-upside-down. Some have agreed with the Russian scholar Bakhtin that popular culture was by such practices essentially subversive and masking, while others have pointed out that for a long while carnival was not exclusively popular but was participated in by all members of the

41

community, elites and masses alike. Many feasts of fools originated in abbeys or cathedrals, although others betray a curious mixture of pagan and Christian themes. Festivities often led to brawls and sometimes serious disorders and, conversely, popular disorders often took on a carnivalesque atmosphere.

Carnival is an excellent focal point for the study of popular beliefs and superstitions. So too is witchcraft. Although the extent of witchcraft has been vastly exaggerated by historians, its incidence in the form of trials being far less than that of murder, its web of superstitions reveals much about values and beliefs. Magical practices and beliefs were indeed widespread, and the credence given to evil magic was merely a corollary of faith in good magic, just as belief in the devil was strengthened by belief in God. Superstitions manifested themselves on numerous occasions. St John's Eve provided Thomas Platter with an example for his journal:

> In the evening we went to Perols to sleep. There were Saint John's fires burning before every door, and people danced around them, or leapt over them, as they do around the carnival fires in Basle. Afterwards each person takes away a pinch of the ashes, which are supposed to possess a host of virtues. In the morning we crossed the lagoon by boat to see the bathers. A crowd of people come and plunge into the sea on St John's Eve, and on the day itself, in the belief that this will protect them from many maladies from which they otherwise would not escape.

Here is a splendid example of a pagan occasion, now Christianized, still revealing popular superstitions which were ultimately at odds with the Christian faith, even if the populace perceived no conflict of conscience on this issue. The medieval church had never succeeded in properly inculcating into the people theological beliefs and had contented itself with merely Christianizing older practices. On the other hand, everyday life was also full of instances of Christian rituals serving 'pagan' purposes. At the edge of a field might be a cross whose shadow would protect the crop; numerous chapels existed in every locality for patron saints who might act as intercessors, providing that the appropriate rituals or pilgrimages were performed. This local or popular religion was functional and animist. It was a system of rituals, ceremonies and superstitions, comprehensive in itself, which helped to explain the world. Like the popular culture with which it was inextricably bound up, it was partly a complex of older beliefs and partly the spontaneous creation of the people. Because the culture was a whole and because it provided an integral vision and explanation of the world, the populace was not very receptive to the high theology of the reform movements of the sixteenth century, the Protestant and Catholic Reformations. Until the late seventeenth century the priests themselves were ignorant, lax and quite incapable of educating their parishioners in the tenets of the faith.

In the long term, however, the Catholic Reformation was to produce the most profound changes in the ways of life and thought of all classes in French society. Partly as a result of a corrupted and inefficient church and in conjunction with other currents in society, the Protestant and Catholic Reformations of the sixteenth century expressed a profound desire for a more ordered and personal religion. Theological debate was crucial, but, leaving to one side the complicated doctrinal issues, we should follow Delumeau (1977) in emphasizing the overall effects of the reform. For the first time the church began effectively to set its house in order and put itself in a position to Christianize the people in a systematic way. This involved first of all a reform of the institutions of the church itself: seminaries were to be set up to train priests, new ecclesiastical orders were founded, missionary work was carried out all over France to root out errors and teach the catechism, and educational establishments were set up for the better off.

This enormous labour was intended to inculcate the basic tenets of the faith and it was to be a work of centuries, not decades. Although the Council of Trent ended in 1563, the wars of religion and the French legal system delayed the acceptance of its decrees until the seventeenth century. Not until the middle of that century did the real work of predication begin, in the wake of famous reformers like Carlo Borromeo, François de Sales and Vincent de Paul. Missionaries such as the R.P. Maunoir toured France drawing huge crowds to their sermons, but the effect was usually temporary and constant pressure was needed if the population was not to lapse into old errors again. The more literate and wealthy classes were quickly receptive to the new currents, both in Protestantism and Catholicism. On the other hand, Jansenism, a most austere form of Catholicism, was for a long time limited in its appeal to the educated Parisian elite of the seventeenth century. Only when combined with an extraordinary manifestation of popular religion, the convulsionary movement of the 1730s, did it widen its appeal to the lower orders.

The accent in the reforms was upon a more personal relationship with God, and the church strongly condemned all those legacies of the animist, 'pagan' tradition formerly accepted by priests. This meant that war was declared by the church upon many aspects of popular culture. Not only were priests required to conform to higher standards of education and morality, but so too were their parishioners, encouraged by exhortations from the pulpit and threats of torments in purgatory. Significantly, the sources left by the ecclesiastical authorities reveal a constant emphasis upon repression, a repression that was uncompromising, insensitive and, partly for those reasons, only partially successful. The struggle was to be a long one and the results are difficult to measure. Historians are sure only of outward conformity by the masses by the eighteenth century, and probably only the nineteenth century witnessed

43

the success of the Catholic Reformation in the countryside – but by then it could only be a partial success because the Revolution had reinforced anti-clericalism amongst Frenchmen.

If the reformation of religion ultimately forced an important change in attitude upon all levels of society, the literate classes were subjected to additional currents. Theirs was the world of humanism and the Renaissance, the rediscovery of classical scholarship and, gradually, the development of a new intellectual framework. By the end of the sixteenth century the growth of lay education in Jesuit schools put the new erudition within reach of the social elite. Yet what really made the Renaissance the preserve of all was the impact of printing. By the early seventeenth century every major town had a press, and by 1700 there were over 350 printing firms in France publishing and republishing a vast array of literature. From outside France came subversive propaganda and forbidden books eagerly acquired by the wealthier reading public. Inside France much of the production was religious, largely catechisms and lives of saints, for such was the taste, but belles lettres and classical texts formed a significant proportion of the total. The education in colleges was based on rhetoric, with emphasis upon the study and imitation of classical models. Not surprisingly, the literature of the seventeenth century is rather dominated by concerns with honour, reputation, virtue, nobility and the idea of *race* (noble lineage), still rooted in medieval conceptions, but given a new humanist emphasis. Neoplatonism and Neostoicism were powerful philosophies which expressed the desire for self-control and order, also advocated by counter-reformation theology and the emergent state. A mid-seventeenth-century library would have contained a mixture of classical works, especially Tacitus, Seneca and Cicero, those of the humanists, Rabelais, Montaigne, Lipsius, theological tracts and some contemporary literature mostly by writers long since forgotten. At the same time, amongst many intellectuals a new spirit of enquiry and criticism was leading to discoveries that were destined to undermine the educated world view of the Renaissance. Scepticism and rationalism gradually became, with Descartes' principles, a method against whose assault the traditional world order could not long survive. The seeds of the dissolution of the Renaissance world view were being sown, but the harvest was not reaped until the early eighteenth century.

The Enlightenment – such an imprecise term – did not by any means gain all educated minds in a day. As a method it became a part of educated culture by the 1750s, but as a set of social and political doctrines its reception was more limited than is often thought. Certainly, the world of provincial academies and the Parisian salons was dominated, by the late eighteenth century, by new ideas and new ideologies, but the intellectual life of small provincial towns remained only slightly affected by the new currents until the Revolution. The bourgeoisie, whose chief aspiration was still to acquire the life-style and dignity of a noble, was

44

not yet very receptive to new ideas which, ironically enough, found the most sympathetic ears amongst the court and Parisian nobility. Caution is required with such generalizations, for it is extremely hard for historians to measure the diffusion of Enlightenment thought beyond those groups which demonstrably purchased the books of the philosophers. Servants and Grub Street hacks may have diffused new doctrines as far down the social scale as the urban artisans. Nevertheless, the Enlightenment was in many respects statist and anti-revolutionary, and few members of the elite espoused the most radical political doctrines. Although the traditional conceptions of power and authority were being slowly eroded, until 1789 most Frenchmen continued to believe in the church and the absolute monarchy.

What is clear is that from at least the mid seventeenth century onwards the literate classes were in a quite different cultural world from that of the lower orders. Education, religion and the emphasis on social distinctions inclined the wealthy to withdraw from popular culture, which they often now disdained. Indeed, popular traditions and mentalities came to be regarded with genuine incomprehension, as part of a different culture. During the eighteenth century the elite of society, still localized and provincial in its outlook, and often hostile to the encroachments of the state, became progressively more homogeneous. Mental horizons expanded to include notions of the state, Europe and extra-European civilizations. Particularism and provincialism remained powerful sentiments, but now it was a question of accepting the albeit limited royal authority and exploiting the political system to advantage.

3 Politics and Administration

For most historians, the ancien régime has been synonymous with the monarchy and its institutions. However, it should be reiterated that when institutions are studied in isolation from the patterns of thought and the prevailing economic and social conditions, a distorted picture may be painted of their nature. In the wake of a mass of new research completed over the last two decades it is now possible to view the monarchy in the context of other aspects of the régime. It emerges as less modern and more deeply rooted in the society of its time. Even when king and ministers were attempting to transform the state and society, they continued to share most of the assumptions of their contemporaries. We must, therefore, beware of the anachronism implied by viewing the rise of the early modern state in the nineteenth-century context of bureaucracy and centralization. The seventeenth-century state was still far closer to the medieval world than it was to the modern one. More realistically, instead of focusing principally upon the rise of the state, we should try to understand how it was that society and ideas modelled and conditioned the development of monarchical institutions. In contrast to the orthodox views expounded in the Introduction, views burdened with nineteenth-century assumptions, this chapter is designed to explain the state in the light of the conclusions reached in other areas of history.

As we have seen, according to St Paul, all temporal power came from God. Kings were God's lieutenants on earth and so had a sacred quality and a duty to defend the true (Catholic) religion. God was the supreme judge, and so too was the king in earthly matters. In popular tradition these qualities had been exhibited in exemplary fashion by St Louis in the thirteenth century and they were still emphasized by the coronation ceremony until the end of the régime. The popular juristic definition of kingship had scarcely altered since the Middle Ages. In 1610 Loyseau put into words what had been believed for a long time, namely that there were five regalian rights: the king could make laws, create offices, decide upon peace and war, have the final decision in judicial matters and mint money. The right to tax people without their consent remained contentious because many continued to believe that the king should live off his own estates. Additionally, and fundamentally, because God had instituted rulers for the benefit of mankind, kings had a duty to defend the commonwealth and protect the life and security of their subjects. Monarchical states need continuity between rulers, for even if they are apparently absolute when they die their laws should die with them, and a fiction had developed that the king never died: 'the king is dead, long live the king!' In this way the royal office passed without interruption through the male line, and thus jurists solved the problem of the continuity or lapse of royal legislative acts over succeeding generations. In addition to its theoretical attributes, French kingship was a dynastic affair, in which the interests of the royal family clearly counted for as much as any regalian duties.

A detailed study of foreign (or dynastic?) policy is beyond the scope of this short book; suffice it to say that the monarchs were forging and fashioning a state responsive to their will. They were intent upon rounding it out, making it more defensible, never willingly ceding territory and always prepared to acquire it. In domestic policy, notions such as a set of fundamental laws regulating the monarchy were never explicitly accepted by the monarchs, as to do so would have limited their authority. For their sovereignty was absolute, it was undivided and not subject to limitations. Quite what the practical implications of this doctrine were will be discussed at a later stage. Clearly, it did not imply the unrestricted exercise of power.

To protect their own interests and those of their subjects, and so fulfil their monarchical duties, the kings had evolved certain judicial, financial and administrative structures. Most of these had made their first appearance during the thirteenth and fourteenth centuries, during the period of strengthening royal power before the Hundred Years War. Often built upon pre-existing areas of administration, either feudal or religious, these institutions had created a stable, if complex, administrative geography by the sixteenth century. By the era of the ancien régime the same institutions had acquired a time-honoured legitimacy and apparent immutability. In this sense the ancien régime had its roots in the Middle Ages.

The two facets of internal government were judicial and fiscal. From the twelfth century the king delegated powers of justice to bailiffs (or senechals in the south) and their jurisdictions numbered about 400 in 1788. The courts presided over by these judges and administrators not only dealt with some cases in the first instance but were also courts of appeal from the *prévôtés* (lower courts in decline by the sixteenth century) and the 70,000 or so seigneurial courts. These were the first organs of state-building in the provinces, by virtue of the wide definition of judicial power, which was not simply the right to judge contentious issues but also included regulative authority and the right to execute decisions. In effect, the crown was exploiting its judicial authority in order to extend and enforce its power over feudal lords.

By the early modern period, by far the most influential bodies in the realm were the royal parlements in the provinces and in Paris. They

47

were final courts of appeal from lower courts and for this reason were known as sovereign courts. The first parlement appeared in the late fourteenth century in Paris and had a jurisdiction over about two-fifths of France, but other sovereign courts were created as the monarchy developed and as new territories were added. Parlements were set up in Languedoc (1434), Dauphiné (1453), Bordeaux (1462), Burgundy (1477), Provence (1501) and Brittany (1553). By the late seventeenth century they numbered thirteen. Some were remodelled ducal or provincial courts in areas that had previously been independent of France, and they therefore continued both to represent the interests of the province and to act as agents of the crown. By virtue of that nebulous concept of *police* they were both judicial and administrative bodies with wide local responsibilities. With powers to preserve public order, they had authority over highways, municipalities, charitable institutions, the grain trade and many other areas of provincial life. They could issue administrative rulings which, if not contradicted by the royal council, eventually became part of the local legal corpus. Like all corporate bodies they had their own traditions and a very strong sense of their own importance, even going so far as to regard themselves as the guardians of the legal forms of the monarchy, and they often compared themselves to Roman senators. These pretensions stemmed from their classical education as magistrates and from their duty to verify and register all royal edicts before they became law. Thus, in a way that was typical of the ancien régime, the lack of a precise definition of their role gave them some influence in the legislative process. This was to be the basis of endless disputes with the royal council over specific laws and sometimes questions of policy. Naturally, the crown never explicitly recognized their powers of interference as constituting a right either of resistance or a legislative attribute.

At the pinnacle of the judiciary was the highest court of the realm, which was the royal council. The king in council was of course the final judge of particularly contentious matters and the council had the right to revoke cases from inferior jurisdictions. In this the king was fulfilling his traditional role and duty.

Other powers existed in the provinces which also played an important role in the administration. Royal governors represented the king and were invested with military powers as well as civil authority. Often they continued in the footsteps of local potentates and they were invariably grand aristocrats. Although some were rebellious, most were loyal, and the decline in their powers was neither so swift nor so complete as was once thought. It is true that by the late seventeenth century many governorships had become sinecures, but this was not so in frontier provinces. Until the end of the ancien régime, even when they were non-resident, they remained important channels of influence and patronage, smoothing relations between centre and periphery.

In many areas, usually those most recently incorporated into the kingdom, provincial estates existed. These represented the three orders of the province which, on the one hand, attempted to safeguard provincial liberties against the crown, and on the other, voted taxation and carried out numerous administrative tasks. The estates of Languedoc and Brittany were particularly powerful and were capable of resisting the monarchy even during the eighteenth century. Although some assemblies disappeared during the seventeenth century, in general the cooperation of the provincial estates was too valuable for the monarchy to do without them, as they had the confidence of the province. This cooperation made the royal administration and collection of taxes an easier task. Ministers were obliged to work through the estates, managing them, threatening them, and bribing them, confirming provincial liberties in return for services. This view constitutes a significant modification to the orthodoxy which stresses the decline of estates.

Even if administrative and judicial issues could sometimes prove contentious at the higher levels in society, the need for justice meant that the institutions were generally well respected. This was not the case with the financial agencies which were imposed on the region by a monarchy in need of ever-increasing sums to finance first wars and then its own wider functions. As Meuvret has shown, fiscal demands did not accord with the popular vision of the monarchy, and its financial agents and institutions were therefore unpopular.

Except in the *pays d'états*, for fiscal purposes, France was divided into *élections*, originating in the mid fourteenth century. Their size varied enormously but they numbered about 100 in 1500 and 179 in 1789. It was possible to tax the *pays d'élections* more heavily than the *pays d'états* where the representative institutions kept alive a stronger sense of identity and privilege, but attempts to introduce *élections* into the *pays d'états* were unsuccessful. In 1630 Provence revolted when the attempt was made. The *pays d'états* on the periphery, therefore, retained their own financial organizations run by the periodic assemblies of the estates. In the *élections* the officers, known as *élus*, were responsible for apportioning the tithe between the communities and judging disputes that might arise. On appeal, these disputes could be carried to the *cours des aides* which specialized in financial matters and were, like the parlements, sovereign courts. The highest level of administration was represented by the treasurers who headed *bureaux des finances* and collected the sums. They often profited sufficiently from their position to become local bankers and could even lend the crown its own money!

At its lowest level, the system consisted of (often unwilling) tax collectors in the villages and the receivers of the tithes. But there was also an ever-multiplying number of agents for the farming and collection of indirect taxes. There were bailiffs and archers to force people to pay; those who manned the barriers at town gates to levy dues on imported goods, or at the tollgates on bridges, roads and rivers; those who had bureaux for the levying of taxes on stamped paper, drinks, windows, carriages; finally, there was the host of officials whose job it was to collect and enforce the hated tax on salt in most areas of France and prevent what was almost an industry, the smuggling of salt from exempt areas to taxed ones. The indirect taxes were farmed out by the government to bodies like the Farmers General, a group which advanced money to the crown and then kept the difference between the price of the Farm and the amount subsequently collected. This may seem to have been an unprofitable option for the royal treasury, but it had the merit of avoiding administration and ensuring money in advance (in an age when regular finance and credit were at a premium).

With the proceeds from the direct and indirect taxes and the substantial income from the sale of office, the government was able to acquire sufficient sums to survive the almost constant wars of the seventeenth century. Nevertheless, Bonney has revealed just how precarious was the financial situation and how near bankruptcy the state often was. On several occasions in the sixteenth and seventeenth centuries and, finally, with the chamber of justice in 1716 and Law's System, the government had recourse to disguised and partial bankruptcies. From the 1630s until the 1700s the weight of direct royal taxation increased almost constantly and often dramatically, while indirect levies and borrowing spiralled upwards even faster. 'The financing of French intervention in the Thirty Years War was an elaborate structure built up very largely on paper transactions' (Bonney, 1981, p. 175). Ultimately, most of the specie came from the 20 million peasants who could barely afford to pay. Resistance to taxation came from peasants and traditionally minded officers who were suspicious of the innovations in fiscal policy and found themselves ever more pressed.

Resistance was so strong in the seventeenth century that to observe and coerce the fiscal administrations it became necessary to introduce a new level of royal agents. These were given wide powers to enable them to maximize the tax yield and quell disorders. They were the royal intendants, who made their first appearance as special commissioners late in the sixteenth century for specific tasks, but who became generalized in the provinces after 1635. Since financial issues were the most important ones for the government, the intendants were destined to become the most powerful royal agents by the eighteenth century. Indeed, they usurped the powers of some financial officials, drastically reducing the role of the *élus* and the *trésoriers*. Although they too were royal judges, unlike other officers they held their powers directly from the royal council and were therefore more responsive to policy decisions and more bureaucratic in their methods. To this extent we may agree with the traditional view.

However, since the nineteenth century much research has been carried out on the intendants and many controversies have arisen. As we have seen in the Introduction, the orthodox view was that they were all-powerful agents of centralization with wide and effective administrative powers, and that they curtailed the influence of the aristocratic governors. This view has been challenged both by investigations of their origins and by studies on their actual administrative activities. Many of the posts owed their origins to requests from provincial governors for judicial officers, and several governors even recommended their own agents for these special commissions (Harding, 1978). They were, therefore, not always, or even usually, at loggerheads with the governors, as has so often been suggested; on the contrary, they usually cooperated well with them. Thus, they were not intended to play a part in curtailing the power of the higher nobility – in fact, they were often clients of aristocratic factions at court. Even so, the ministers usually found them to be the most efficient agents available, and consequently heaped new tasks upon them. Unfortunately, after Colbert's reorganization of their role they had quite simply so much to do that it was impossible for them to fulfil all of their duties. Even in the face of ministerial disapproval they recruited sub-delegates to assist them, but these men were usually local office-holders and had divided loyalties, were always unpaid and were themselves lacking in resources.

The intendants became the eyes and ears of the central administration, writing endless long reports on local conditions in reply to constant demands for information. Although historians have found the reports of the intendants to be a mine of information, especially a series written in 1698 to instruct the king's grandson on the condition of France, they are of variable quality and exactitude. In truth, even the intendants had disadvantages as well as advantages, for they were far from being entirely modern administrators. It was easy for them to distort information to protect clients, hard for them to choose between enforcing royal policy and defending the interests of the province, and tempting for them to paint a rosy picture of their administration in order to create a good impression, advance their career and move back to Paris or on to a more prestigious province. Even the intendants were not ideal agents of centralization.

One French historian, F.-X. Emmanuelli, after having completed a lengthy study of the intendancy of Provence, has vigorously attacked the myth of the intendant. There is 'a stereotype of the French intendant . . . that of an all powerful individual, the foremost agent of absolutism and of unification (in the manner of the Third Republic) as it would be understood in the nineteenth century, the force behind the transformations in the provinces during the eighteenth century'. This myth emerged during the nineteenth century as a validation of a certain historical method: 'the institutional text taken as really describing the actual experience of life, the constituted authority as proof of existence in space and time, the example assumed to be of general validity. By virtue of which one was logically excused both from trying to go beneath the surface to explore the deeper workings of the intendancy, and from attempting to make a true assessment of their effective powers'. The intendants had derisory financial support for their work: 0.3 per cent of state receipts for the administration, and 1.3 per cent of pensions accorded. Furthermore, the central direction of the intendants is largely illusory. 'From 1744 to 1790 there was not a single royal decree particular to Provence which had not been requested or even drafted by the intendant in Aix-en-Provence.' And for the most part the intendants merely repeated the opinions and even the words of their sub-delegates, who were so closely integrated into local society. And, finally, they proved quite incapable of solving the problem of debt (of which Pagès made so much in his assessment) right down to the end of the régime (Emmanuelli, 1981). M. Bordes has shown how some intendants were, like the foremost example of Turgot in Limoges, enlightened reformers in their region. But many others, such as Fontanieu in Dauphiné, were almost entirely preoccupied with the state of the military roads, public order and the provision of money for state coffers. Such differences mean that the relationship of the intendants to centralization is likely to remain a subject of controversy for some time to come.

It is difficult to know where to fit the church into an explanation of the politics and administration of the monarchy. On the one hand, it played an important but neglected role in the administration of France, and provided a certain revenue to the monarchy, while on the other hand, it was an independent institution in a very ambiguous relationship with the temporal powers. Although it was ostensibly spiritual in function, the Gallican church had developed temporal interests which made it the most powerful corporation in France. It owned at least 10 per cent of the land and had a well-organized and efficiently bureaucratic financial structure. Its revenue from the tithe was enormous and it was certainly undertaxed. Every five years its assembly of clergy voted a 'free gift' to the king to assist his finances, and its financial security enabled it to provide the crown with huge sums in the form of loans. Typically, the royal treasury allowed these to accumulate, unrepaid, to the extent that in 1789 the church was indebted on behalf of the monarchy. The church had its own courts, using canon law, and it controlled the universities, while most other educational establishments were run by ecclesiastical orders, and the parish schools were run by the curés. Thus the church carried out many of the tasks which would later be adopted by state organizations in the nineteenth century, but which only the most enlightened thinkers of the eighteenth century conceived of as being within the proper sphere of state activity.

Throughout our period, the higher clergy had a role to play in government. Bishops and archbishops helped to control their dioceses on behalf of the civil powers. In 1707 Bishop Fleury organized the defence of Provence against invasion, and J.F. de la Marche was a noted administrative bishop in Brittany (Sée, 1927). There was, in fact, a whole breed of administrative bishops who worked with the upper echelons of the provincial administration. In the provincial estates the presidency of a prestigious archbishop – of Narbonne in Languedoc for example – was, with the support of the other ecclesiastical delegates, often a crucial factor in their control. One historian has written, 'Even outside the assemblies, the bishops still played a considerable role: installed at the head of the diocesan bureaucracy, they were expected to direct the financial administration of their diocese; and, what is more, to judge from their correspondence, they appear to have been every bit as well informed about the temporal interests of their flock as of the spiritual' (Du Bouëtzies de Kerougouen). Even at the lowest level, the parish was usually the area adopted as a civil administrative division and the curé was expected to read out edicts from the pulpit. In the confessional, he would encourage, through the redefinition of sin and moral duty, the payment of taxes and obedience to the temporal powers. In fact, church and state were hand in hand. By the sixteenth century the monarchy had secured control over ecclesiastical appointments and, although Louis XIV failed to browbeat the pope in the quarrel over the *régale*, the balance was generally favourable to the monarchy. The church of the Catholic Reformation and the baroque state pursued many of the same ideals: order and hierarchy were as important to one as to the other. Church and state were completely interrelated and this relationship was a part of the peculiar flavour of the ancien régime.

Over the royal bureaucracy presided the king and his ministers in the council of state. Before 1547 it was more informal than formal and simply took place in the context of the royal household. In that year a ruling called together certain princes, cardinals, grand officers of the crown and secretaries responsible for finance 'to hold the King's counsel and discuss questions of state and finance, and upon these matters give advice upon the order and provision which must be made, for the better understanding of the King so that he may make known his royal pleasure'. Over the next eighty years the council became a bureaucratic institution with permanent secretaries and councillors of state. The growth in the council and its eventual subdivision into new councils of finance, despatches and justice (1630) reflected the increasing competence and complexity of the developing monarchical state. Although the councils existed in separate forms and met on different days of the week, in theory they all constituted only one council over which the monarch presided. Decisions on policy were taken, rulings issued and contentious matters discussed or judged. From the seventeenth century, the secretaries of state began to enter into immense quantities of increasingly detailed correspondence. In many cases their archives have survived both the Revolution and the vagaries of family papers to provide us with the most important documentation on the nature and functions of the régime. Tragically, one source that has disappeared is the minutes of the council of state. These would have enlightened us on the details and nature of the discussions in the royal presence. It is therefore not known whether the kings really decided for themselves against the advice of councillors or followed the opinion of the majority. Nor can we assess with accuracy the influence of informally given but undoubtedly important advice received from other trusted courtiers before meetings.

A neat and schematized version of the bureaucratic structure should not mislead us about the way power really worked. 'The history of institutions is not history properly speaking; it is the description of the conditions of a power apparatus at a given moment, a description which ignores its genesis, and which in particular disregards the tumultuous reality contained within it', wrote the brilliant Spanish historian J. Vicens Vives. It is important to realize that we are not dealing with an administrative state capable of wielding power effectively through its bureaucratic agencies alone. Of course, it must be recognized that the power and effectiveness of the state did increase greatly during the seventeenth and eighteenth centuries. The state took on a wider range of functions, it gradually succeeded in preserving a greater level of public order, and it was successful in collecting vastly augmented sums of money from the population. Nevertheless, if anachronism is to be avoided, the baroque state should not be viewed as a slightly less efficient version of the bureaucratic state of the nineteenth century. The absolute monarchy was deeply rooted in its own history and far too many conceptual, legal and physical impediments existed for it to have any chance of working as a centralized modern bureaucracy. Until the mid eighteenth century, it operated within a medieval or Renaissance world view and was imbued with ethics quite foreign to the enlightened, liberal, constitutional state which was to succeed it. In order to appreciate the specificity of the ancien régime monarchy it is necessary to consider in greater detail the wide range of checks upon the exercise of monarchical power. In this area the orthodox view of the development of the monarchy has been subjected to the heaviest criticism. Against the doctrine of the institutional historians it should be argued that there was no successful transition to an administrative monarchy after Colbert. So little evidence has been put forward to substantiate their argument that it is astonishing it should have survived for so long. Such a view is an illusion created by placing too great an emphasis upon institutional records.

There was a large measure of support for monarchical rule. The monarchy provided ideological legitimation and it was seen to be fulfilling a necessary role in society. Without popular consent its coercive power would have been too limited for it to survive these troubled centuries: in cases of flagrant disobedience there were few options open to the crown. There was an extremely inefficient force of archers to enforce law and order in the countryside, and towns had their bourgeois militia and the watch, but there were no state organizations except the judiciary. The army was the only real force which could be called upon to quell disorders, but it could never be a permanent instrument of rule. Even when a standing army existed after the 1630s it was itself a source of disorder and was usually too involved in foreign war to be available for large-scale repressive acts. It could be used in exemplary fashion, as in Brittany in 1675 when the peasant revolt was savagely punished, but such measures were infrequent because they were expensive. Most disorders broke out in wartime, exactly when the physical resources of the monarchy were most stretched, and subsided before troops arrived. Without the moral authority of the church and the tacit consent of the population, the bureaucracy could never have administered France.

A fundamental restriction upon monarchical power was the poor network of communications. Roads were extremely bad and most were little more than tracks that were impassable in bad weather. On many occasions it was safer to strike out across fields than keep to treacherous roads. Rural communities and provincial towns existed in a degree of isolation which barely altered until the eighteenth century. Finally, for military, economic and political reasons, the central government began to organize the construction of a better network. In some areas decisive progress was made after 1738 when labour dues, the *corvée*, were extended throughout the realm. Even so, France was an extremely large state with forests, mountains and marshy areas of difficult access. It took at least a week for a courier to reach the south from Versailles, while travellers could expect to take three weeks by coach. In such conditions the government simply remained in ignorance of local events, so that delay and the evasion of commands was easy.

Such isolation, and the different historical experiences of many provinces, had resulted in the wide range of regional life-styles, legal codes and corporate bodies which together formed cultural and legal barriers to the extension of monarchical power. Far from being in a position to weld these varied provinces and localities into a unified whole, the monarchy, in periods of weakness, had actually been obliged to guarantee the liberties of provinces, towns and corporations against its own further pressure. During this period it was almost axiomatic that no institution could be suppressed. Instead, its privileges would be left intact and it would be encouraged to fall into abeyance, overshadowed by a new body with wider powers. When, in the second half of the eighteenth century, the monarchy began to suppress or remodel institutions such as the municipalities, parlements or guilds, it was treading on dangerous ground. Above all, the French monarchy was legitimate, and this meant that it had to respect the law as well as make it. To act in an arbitrary illegal manner without respect for tradition and privilege was to invite accusations of despotism and to risk undermining the aura of kingship.

In these circumstances it was almost impossible to issue an edict with general applications which would not run into stiff resistance on good legal grounds from some area of France. In 1549 a successful provincial revolt prevented the government from extending the salt tax into Guyenne. In the 1760s the municipal reforms of the controller general Laverdy required regional variations and exemptions. Resistance to the reform by municipal oligarchies was strong enough to provide a pretext for the abandonment of the whole project in 1771, when the sale of new municipal offices was again adopted as a financial expedient. Detailed case studies of such situations, for example a study of Colbert's failure to introduce maritime conscription in Brittany (Asher, 1960), tell us a great deal about the nature of the régime. According to one contemporary, flexibility was part of the very definition of a good minister. It was essential that he should understand the need to deal with the various provinces in his department in a manner which took account of their differing customs and laws, and he should consequently be prepared to accept modifications to the execution of general policies or particular rulings.

Long before nationalism formed an essential aspect of the *mentalité* of the population, provincialism and corporatism were powerful sentiments. In politics and administration the corporate ideology was one of the most significant impediments both to reform and to efficient administration. The dignity, honour and status of an individual office-holder was ultimately bound up with the prestige, authority and jurisdiction of his corps. In the context of overlapping jurisdictions, the absence of clear definitions of the power of institutions, and the importance of precedent in society, this mentality meant that there were perpetual quarrels between the various judicial authorities. People bringing suits would naturally appeal to the court most likely to favour their case, so both parties might appeal to a different court. This then enabled the courts to intervene on good grounds and defend or extend their jurisdiction. The fact that many cases might have both a simple judicial aspect and a financial one permitted endless disputes between the fiscal and the judicial courts. The *cours des aides* and the parlements were often in dispute, while the intendants found the parlements particularly obstructive to their pretensions. The parlements were constantly intervening in ecclesiastical jurisdiction through the system of appeals to the lay courts. In turn, they were repeatedly obliged to defend their own jurisdiction against the revocation of cases to the royal council. Many of these disputes recurred generation after generation, and some of them lasted for more than a generation!

The venal bureaucracy has been appraised by historians in several different ways, partly because the office-holders usually had a number of foci for their loyalty. First and foremost came not their post but their family and friends, followed by their clients and patrons, and the interest of their corps, town and province. Many of them would be open to self-interest and manipulation, and their practices often conflicted with the demands of royal administration. Tax collectors would sometimes make shameless profits, favour their friends or be subjected to pressure from powerful landowners to underassess them, while magistrates would often favour their patrons. A striking instance of the use to which a powerful judicial post could be put is provided by the case of the first president of the parlement of Normandy in the 1640s. Theoretically the first representative of the king in the court, he exploited his post to build up a network of clients and form a 'veritable cabal'. The president was honest when friends were not involved in cases, but, observed a contemporary, 'when it was a question of his interests or that of his friends, he did not know what justice was. By the support which he gave to his friends, this entirely relative honesty had made him into the most powerful man of the robe in parlement and in the whole province'.

All localities were ruled by elites which intermarried and whose horizons rarely extended much beyond the province. Genealogies, family record books and memoirs reveal how local dynasties were formed and how they built up their power over generations by the acquisition of offices and astute marriage alliances. In the 1660s the family of the future Cardinal de Fleury had one member in the *cour des aides*, another was a treasurer general of the province, while daughters married into families of similar influence. The same social mechanism which created local elites could also lead to the formation of a political class loyal to the monarchy. The masters of requests, from whom intendants were recruited, were, from the mid seventeenth century, practically all Parisian in origin (80 per cent). They were, of course, all noble, rich, and, by the eighteenth century, almost all related. Marriage alliances were important for politics as well as for social mobility. It has often been noted that the rise of Colbert was not so much the rise of an individual as the final triumph of a clan. Many an example could be given, especially in the seventeenth century, of corporate resistance to royal policy generated as much by threatened factional interests as by corporate or constitutional motives. Evidence of this is now likely to lead to much rewriting of what were previously seen as principally constitutional disputes. We shall see how, after the Fronde, the central government learned to compromise with the local elites in order to operate a less-contentious system of government.

Paradoxically, perhaps the most effective counterweight to the forces of resistance lay in the traditions of the venal bureaucracy. If it was not a nineteenth-century bureaucracy, or a modern one, it was an administration of sorts. The office-holders obviously carried with them their social and political conceptions derived from other areas of life, but this should not blind us to the fact that the French bureaucracy was for a long time the envy and the model of Europe. Certainly it had its limitations, and these were difficult to rectify. Richelieu observed that the perfect republic would not have venality of office, but that it was financially impossible for the monarchy to repurchase offices. As Pagès wrote: 'We do not give sufficient consideration to the fact that venality of office had become, in the seventeenth century, an essential element in the political and social structure of the kingdom and that in suppressing it, one would have shaken the whole edifice' (Pagès, 1932b, p. 493). Nevertheless, the advantages outweighed the disadvantages. A reasonably efficient administration was provided at a fairly low cost to the state. In effect, salaries were not paid at all, for the *gage* was an interest payment on the value of the loan to the state, which was the capital invested in the office. Venality was not only a notion of public office rooted in the medieval conception of property, it was also a system of government credit! The receipts from the sale of office were enormous and were an essential means of acquiring money from the wealthier classes normally protected from direct taxation by exemptions. By accepting the proprietorial concept of office the crown was eventually able to build up an administration which had high traditions of service within the usual functions of the office. Fathers gave sons training in the duties of the office they were to inherit, while family honour or the corporate spirit required loyalty to the monarchy. Given a modicum of pressure from the king, officers would carry out their tasks reasonably conscientiously in normal circumstances. They would only become recalcitrant, grossly inefficient and dilatory when new and threatening tasks were required of them, or when they felt their position being undermined. Ultimately, the office stemmed from the royal prerogative, and this fact imposed a limit upon resistance to royal commands. Unless circumstances made royal retribution quite out of the question, there was always the possibility that the crown could deprive individuals of their charges and try them for lèse-majesté. Officers might quarrel with the monarchy about the distribution of power within the kingdom, but they could never go so far as to oppose the monarchy as an institution. Thus, within limits, and in the context of the early modern set of ethics, the crown possessed a reasonably efficient bureaucracy. As the internal disorders subsided from the mid seventeenth century, resistance too died down. The venal bureaucracy came to realize that the balance of power had shifted in favour of the central government. The rules of the political game were now different. It had become a question of securing the greatest advantage for self and locality from the system. For this reason the tone of correspondence alters by the eighteenth century as greater obedience and more circumspection developed. The long, slow process of state formation was gradually succeeding, but it was far from complete in 1789.

Only in the last two decades has it become accepted that royal authority, so absolute in theory, was far from being so in practice. In order to explain this, historians for a long time tended to assume that the causes of the failure lay in the budding bureaucracy which, because it was in an early stage of development, was inefficient and sapped its own effectiveness by its failure to curtail privilege and corruption. Unfortunately, this view, although it is convenient in permitting notions of continuity between the early modern state and the more modern, bureaucratic, post-revolutionary state, depends upon the premise that the royal administration did indeed resemble a modern bureaucracy. In one further way it did not. In the modern state the concept of the office determines the nature of a man's function in the administration. In the ancien régime the system was much less well-defined, to the extent that for the higher offices almost the reverse was true: offices were made by indidivuals, and what a man did determined the character of his office. Unfortunately, studies which deal with an office over a long period rarely concentrate sufficiently upon the politics of specific situations and the role of individuals to bring this out. Here is an area in which biography can be helpful. Recent studies of the *lit de justice* and the coronation ceremony have revealed another element, the ancien régime's gift for writing into apparently traditional legal texts variations which had very specific or even accidental origins, thus unwittingly altering the traditional forms in a way which might normally escape attention. The resultant texts can seriously mislead the historian looking for continuities. An example of partly misleading continuities is to be found in the analogy between the intendants and the nineteenth-century prefects in France. It is perfectly legitimate to trace the origins of a modern office back to its antecedents during an earlier form of government, but the different ethics which prevailed in the earlier case should be properly recognized. An office defined in similar ways might function rather differently in different periods and societies according to the prevailing social values, ambitions and ethics.

It is not difficult to argue that the ancien régime saw a system of government in which the nature of the office sometimes bore very little relation to the degree of political influence wielded by its holder. In the central government, which was still the royal household, a first gentleman of the bedchamber might have as much influence over decisions of policy as a secretary of state. However, it is impossible to tell without a detailed study, not of the office, but of the man: he might have acquired the post for purely prestigious reasons, or have been given it as a reward for past services. A family as strong as the Noailles and as well-connected by marriage might, by its accumulation of court offices, governorships and royal favour, be in a position to exercise as much power as a minister. Histories of such families are extremely useful for an appreciation of the finer points of the history of the state. Cardinal Fleury held no ministerial office and yeʋ he had almost complete control over French politics for many years. Moreover, the acquisition of an office might be no more than a reflection of the existing influence of a particular individual. For example, it would be hard to say whether Dubois had a greater part in the formation of policies when he was a *conseiller d'état* in 1720 or when he was *premier ministre* in 1723.

Another important consideration is that the success of a decision by an official depended largely on his own ability to see that it was enforced. In a country which was not well policed there were many ways in which the privileged subordinate officials and the recalcitrant population could avoid cooperation. Much that the royal government ardently desired and even decreed was never implemented in France, and for an intendant or secretary of state to be successful in his functions he could not rely exclusively on the administrative hierarchy. His *crédit* at court, the network of his friends and clients, his prestige and his ability to settle for a negotiated compromise all came into play to increase the effectiveness of his power over his subordinates. Civil obedience to the royal administration was not a deeply rooted habit; it needed to be encouraged and exacted, and many generations of Frenchmen passed before the use of patronage could be suspended and the system described as impersonal and bureaucratic. Although there is a debate about the point at which this transition took place, it was certainly not complete before the end of the nineteenth century.

The use of an example helps to explain the argument. From the 1680s until 1739 Provence had two intendants, a father and his son. The elder Le Bret, in the early years of the century, was no more than a useful aide to the archbishop of Aix and to the military commandant who actually governed the province in the continual absence of the governor. The son, on the other hand was able to control the province quite effectively on his own, because he was by then of the second generation in Provence and he both benefited from the roots his father had put down in the province and inherited the network of clients that he had slowly built up. It is a significant comment upon the power structures in Provence that he also became the first president of the local parlement, and it was this post which facilitated his administration as much as that of intendant. In this situation Villars, the governor from 1713, rarely visited the province and the commandant was of no importance. The conclusion to be drawn is that authority was not necessarily based upon the tenure of a formal office and that the system functioned far from bureaucratically, even after Louis XIV and Colbert. The relative importance of the governor, commandant, archbishop and intendant varied according to circumstances which have to be closely investigated and their power was largely dependent upon their prestige. This was in turn intimately connected with their ability to secure patronage at court and control patronage in the province. Considerable evidence survives of the continuation of such practices until the end of the régime in 1789. In that year the Duc d'Harcourt, governor of Normandy, controlled almost all the votes of the noble representation of his province in the Estates General.

If the system was not wholly bureaucratic, how did it function? Clearly, it was rather more complex than it appeared in the nineteenth century to historians such as Tocqueville. It is now time to draw attention to several elements, all recently emphasized by historians, which should henceforth be incorporated into any explanation of the power structures. Enough evidence has accumulated to constitute a serious challenge to the Whiggish paradigm of administrative/absolutist development from the time of Francis I to Louis XIV and after.

Patronage and clientage is certainly the most important new element to be added to the picture. In the medieval and late Renaissance world, fidelities, patronage and clientage networks have long been recognized as important, but the rise of the state was thought to have eradicated them. Studies by Mousnier on *fidélités*, Ranum on Richelieu and his *créatures*, Harding on provincial governors and Beik on the control of Languedoc have called this decline into question, while Kettering has drawn together much of the material in a general appraisal. If these studies insist upon the importance of clientage and fidelities in the seventeenth century, other studies, including the author's own research, suggest that such links remained important in the eighteenth century.

When trying to analyse patronage and clientage no rigid definition will suffice because so much of it depends upon the aims of both parties. The patron may be interested in political services, while the client, who is usually lower down the social scale, will probably have more social aims or political ones in a more local environment. The essential feature is the rendering of services, often on a long-term basis. Years may elapse before a return favour is called for. This principle of human relations figures prominently in the historical sources for the whole of the ancien régime. Memoirs are full of references to favours owed, expected or received. The archives bearing on the work of every government department contain very many letters pleading for a pension, or the preferment of a son, a friend, or a faithful servant. The antechambers of ministers, prestigious courtiers, commissioners or anyone with control over the distribution of monetary funds or offices in the administration, the church or the army, are known to have been crowded with people asking for some small or large favour, some share in the patron's success. Private letters reveal a constant preoccupation with personal *crédit*, *considération* and rank, while it is generally accepted that marriages among the richer sections of the community were rarely arranged primarily with a view to the happiness of the two individuals but were an alliance of families. Patronage and clientage was both a fundamental mechanism of social and political advancement and a vital aspect of the system of government which exploited it as a technique of control. Most of the patronage networks were centred upon high aristocrats or ministers.

It is now accepted that Richelieu built up a group of creatures whom he used to help him govern. He made himself governor of the troublesome province of Brittany in order to flatter and control the area. Harding has shown how important governors continued to be, and how they proliferated in the seventeenth century. Much later, and therefore more telling perhaps, is the evidence that can be cited to show that in the eighteenth century aristocratic governors, or their equivalent, together with intendants and archbishops, made concerted attempts to use their *créatures* and their ability to secure or withhold favours granted by the king, to ensure that local or provincial estates ran smoothly. It would be a mistake to assume that these assemblies were a mere formality in the eighteenth century – one only has to consult the unofficial records of the estates to see evidence of great care and a good deal of nervousness by the government and its representatives. In 1750 the estates of Languedoc, mishandled, refused the *vingtième* and other taxes too, while the opposition of the Breton estates and parlement in the 1760s is notorious. Throughout the period, it was necessary for the government to exploit the hierarchical social system as an important element in the government of France.

Taken together, these views constitute a serious challenge to the orthodox view of the development of monarchical institutions. It was long believed that the monarchy, trying to establish control over a fragmented, provincialized, localized country in which communications were poor and local elites strong, relied upon the new bourgeoisie in order to emerge pre-eminent over the higher nobility. Now it may be argued, leaving aside all the details and specialized research, that quite a different thing was happening. France did indeed have provincial and local elites, and they existed quite independently of the central government in the sixteenth century. Many areas had centuries of autonomy behind them and powerful aristocrats had large clientage networks in the provinces. For the modern state to emerge, it was first necessary to bring these networks under the control of the king, so that he might exploit them in his favour. There are, as it were, two kinds of government in the modern state: central and local. Both existed during the early modern period, but local government was not yet *seen* as constituting a part of the state, which was itself a new phenomenon. The process at work was, in the very long term, the fusing of these two levels into one chain, ultimately bureaucratic in nature, so that the periphery could be controlled from the centre. Before that happened, what was at work was largely the extension of royal patronage to incorporate the local networks. That is the really effective centralization which is taking place in the seventeenth century. For this task the higher nobility was vital, as these families were either important in the province already, or could be encouraged to set up their own new clientage networks to further the king's business. Bureaucratic centralization was the work of the Revolution and the nineteenth century.

Several excellent and detailed studies exist of the clientage system at work, of which just two may be singled out here. P. Lefebvre (1973) has studied the clientage network of the princes de Condé in the seventeenth century, showing how it worked through the household offices of the princes. By the end of the seventeenth century the objective of the princes had been achieved – a large, unified network of clients existed, linked by marriage and offices. Many of them entered royal service in the administration or became counsellors of state or counsellors in the law courts, especially in Burgundy, of course, where the Condé were provincial governors. Lefebvre has produced tables, compiled principally to demonstrate social ascension, but which also reveal the infiltration of institutions by clients of the princes. As politics by the eighteenth century had changed to working generally *for* the king, even if *against* his ministers, the system functioned as an aid to the government of Burgundy, and to a faction led by the house of Condé. This system remained a dimension of Burgundian politics at least until the death of Condé in 1740. Another especially valuable study is by Dessert and Journet on 'Le Lobby Colbert'. They demonstrate that Colbert constructed a huge network of *créatures*, mostly in the financial sphere, which he used to 'ensure an effective administration of affairs by responding to the difficulties imposed upon him by the nature of the kingdom, with a system of personal relations which was more efficient'. To add to this the present writer's research on the structure of politics shows how the Cardinal de Fleury ensured the success of his religious policy by exploiting the system of ecclesiastical patronage that he controlled (Campbell, 1985). A good illustration of the system at work is to be found in a letter from a client of the Duc de Richelieu in the troublesome provincial parlement of Toulouse, which had been refusing to recognize the duke as an accredited royal agent in 1740.

As I am intent upon finding occasions to demonstrate my zeal and my enormous gratitude for all the favours with which you have honoured me, I have worked all this year to calm the magistrates in the courts about the difficulties which they have given you about the ceremonial for your reception in the town. I have negotiated as best I can with the six or seven principal judges who control the votes of all the others. Finally I believe that I have succeeded so well that one of them came to see me yesterday on behalf of his colleagues and said that they were ready to enter into all the arrangements you desired and that they wished for nothing more than the opportunity to make reparation to you for all the difficulties which they had created.

Why were high aristocrats so important in this sort of role? The answer must be linked to what is known of social attitudes as well as to the role of aristocrats in the royal patronage network. Much of it has to do with ceremony, role-playing and symbolism, all relatively neglected areas in studies of the ancien régime and deserving much closer attention than they have received. Role-playing is the first aspect to consider. The historian searching for accurate descriptions of, for example, Cardinal de Fleury might be misled if he failed to consider the importance of role-playing in public life. Instead of certain traits of character emerging from descriptions of Fleury, there is only a portrait of the perfect cleric – gentle, subtle, modest and so on. He was perceived not so much as an individual, but more as a type. Was not that the secret of his success? He knew how to conform to a social type – just as from afar all parlementaires appeared the same in their red robes, and the Ducs de Noailles or Richelieu, governors of Languedoc, looked not so much like individuals as dukes. It is a far cry from politics today: Noailles almost literally stepped into his father's shoes and in Languedoc was a powerful aristocrat, closer to the king than anyone else in the province could ever be. Like the king, he would sit under a canopy, and, just as for the king, a whole series of approaches through intermediaries was required in order to gain an audience. It all enhanced majesty and sovereignty. Elevated as he was by ceremony, dress, precedent and pre-ordained role, it is no wonder that he had an influence in the estates. Akin to ceremony and role-playing was the exploitation of symbolism by the monarchy. The understanding of certain symbols was a part of life which, however, we no longer find readily accessible. In the ancien régime one would be able to read a painting or a statue by knowing the code – just as today we recognize the symbols of fascism, for example. And for the bigger, more elaborate, ceremonies, descriptions could be purchased, such as Molière's 'Relation de la fête de Versailles' (1683).

Many other practices of the monarchy were significant for government. Guenée and Giesey have evoked the immense propaganda effort of courtly ceremonies in Renaissance France until the reign of Louis XIV, and Ferrier-Caverivière has done much the same for the image of Louis XIV in literature. From the time of Richelieu, through academies and royal patronage, the arts were enlisted in the monarchical cause. In this way, the illusion of absolutism was created in the form of monumental architecture and sculpture. A marble sculpture of Louis XIV trampling the Fronde was situated in the square in the city hall of Paris – although the victory had hardly been an outright one. Public squares were constructed in many provincial towns, often with equestrian statues of the monarch as a centrepiece. Perhaps some of the classical allusions were lost upon the mass of the population, but everyone could interpret the fleur de lys scorched into the flesh of criminals passing by in chain gangs on their way to the galleys, as a symbol of vengeful royal authority. The preambles to royal edicts and Colbertian letters reveal another aspect of the technique of government – straightforward bluff. These other areas of research are perhaps equally as important as patronage for an understanding of state power during this long period. Had France lived under an administrative monarchy after Colbert, such efforts would not have been necessary.

At this point it is well to re-examine the argument. Students of the ancien régime will be quick to point out that few would disagree with this assessment of the structure and operation of the régime up until the time of Mazarin and Colbert, but many would go on to argue that the advent of the intendants and the royal victory over the Frondes, 1648–53, radically altered the picture later in the century. The case for regarding the intendants as all-powerful agents of centralization has been refuted above – at least according to the present state of studies. It remains to discuss the consequences of the Fronde, for the present interpretation would appear to rest upon it. Did those civil wars mark a turning point made possible by an outright royal victory over the higher aristocracy and the parlements, which henceforth permitted the establishment of a more centralized, more bourgeois régime? Until very recently this question has been difficult to answer in detail because there have been so few studies of the immediate aftermath of the wars. One such study is by Hamscher on *The Parlement of Paris after the Fronde*. He reveals that, far from reducing the parlement to obedience by a show of renewed royal authority, Louis XIV and his ministers actually behaved very differently. The ministry carefully avoided causing conflicts, consulted the parlement on legal reforms, allowed it to keep control of recruitment to its own ranks, thus acquiescing in its oligarchical and nepotist tendencies, did not attack its jurisdiction, and left parlementaire privileges intact. Subsequent royal propaganda in edicts, as in 1673, made it appear as if the parlementaire opposition had been silenced. The sudden revival of outspoken opposition over the Jansenist issue in 1713, two years before Louis XIV's death, reveals the continued strength of the courts. Meanwhile, intendants were warned repeatedly, by Colbert himself, not to interfere in the jurisdiction of local institutions and told not to exceed their commissions. Recent work on the royal court has shown how the higher aristocracy retained power in key governorships and in household offices giving access to the patronage powers of the king. Those few peers who were deprived of direct provincial authority were amply compensated by prestigious positions at court which, far from being of trivial importance, in the long run ensured their continued influence in factional politics, as well as permitting a defence of their family interests (Mettam, 1988).

As is now known, the eighteenth century saw peers, parlements and local institutions still in a very strong position in the state. In short, the true impact of the Fronde was to act as an awful warning to the king and his ministers of the dangers of alienating by unwise policies too many authorities at once. By its severity and dangers for the monarchy, the Fronde determined the later response of ministers in the direction of caution, for it exposed the limits to royal authority. The royal victory had been hard won and was in the nature of a compromise. Other sections of French society were also influenced by the struggle: France could not be allowed to slip into civil war again and support for the monarchy was the best guarantee of order. It was thus better to work with the monarchy and seek an accommodation of interests than to risk disaster and defeat. In these ways the Fronde conditioned the development of the régime for many decades. Only in the mid eighteenth century did necessity and a new philosophy push a new generation of ministers towards the disruptive business of fundamental reform.

A whole new area of research has emerged in the last decade which confirms in a detailed and comprehensive manner the view that the state was a partnership between the king and the local and provincial elites. The basis of this partnership was partly power and influence, which has already been discussed, and partly money. In a substantial study, which is a masterpiece of detailed research, Dessert (1984) has revealed the relationship between the courtly landed aristocracy and the financiers who advanced the money for most aspects of government credit. The host of financiers who lent money to the crown had the closest of ties with the leading aristocratic families whose huge landed estates gave them enormous revenue to invest and whose power at court gave them influence to advance clients. Taking a total of 534 out of 693 financiers during the whole reign of Louis XIV, Dessert has shown that there is no truth in the popular contemporary image of the upstart financier whose social origins lay in the lower classes. Most (85 per cent) were office-holders, more than half of whom had a financial office, and 79 per cent were noble. Almost all were Catholic and to succeed it was necessary to be connected by marriage and employment to high society, where the real money lay. Most interesting is the revelation that the basis of their fortune was fragile and that the money for government contracts came largely from the landed elite at court. Most of the loans floated by the government were invested in by the clergy, by municipalities and above all by financiers whose role it was to channel discreetly aristocratic funds into investments that were not considered socially acceptable. The crown needed the supply of hard cash which could only come from the seigneurial class possessing vast estates. Rents and seigneurial dues provided their cash, and the receipts from royal taxes provided the profits for this world of courtly finance. The links were too close and the influences too powerful for ministers (if they had not profited themselves) to investigate corruption in detail. When Mazarin died he left strict instructions that no one should investigate his fortune after his death: 'which my lord orders expressly, because it is his will and there are several things in the accounts which it is very important to keep secret, as much for the well-being of the state as for numerous people and families inside and outside the kingdom'. Persecuting, or merely prosecuting, a financier could be embarrassing for, like Foucquet, he might name names. Dessert concludes that the state was caught up in its own contradictions:

> The state, by virtue of its finances and the whole system secreted by them, was imprisoned by the ties of dependence upon society which its own system had generated. Any attempt to change or challenge the fiscal system, even in the interests of the state, implied a challenge to the society upon which the self-same state was based. Therein lies one of the most serious contradictions in the ancien régime.

If the financial system had been 'captured' by the court aristocracy by the mid seventeenth century, in the provinces increasing royal fiscal demands created the basis for a compromise between the king and the regional élites. In the *pays d'états*, and here Brittany and Languedoc have been studied most closely, the provincial elite was composed of only a few hundred families. By defending local privileges and interests during negotiations over royal financial demands, they were above all anxious to protect themselves. In effect, they allowed the peasants to pay higher taxes in return for the confirmation of provincial liberties which mostly benefited those in positions of power: parlementaires, financial officers, agents of the estates and the municipal oligarchies, who were intermarried. The same families were often involved in the financial organization of tax collection and were able to syphon off, quite legally, as costs of collection, a significant percentage for themselves. Loans by municipalities and estates would be contracted on behalf of the central government and the elites would invest freely, securing a reasonable return in the form of interest payments. In Brittany, in 1736, the sum of 1,497,298 *livres* was budgeted as interest payments out of a total grant by the estates of just over 11 million *livres* for three years. Loans contracted to avoid new taxes in the long term were actually paid for by increased taxes in the short term, mostly levied on the urban and rural poor who had no exemptions. For Languedoc, Beik (1985) has been able to show the development of this partnership after the Fronde. From 1647 to 1677 the proportion of direct taxes collected and retained in various ways by the notables rose from 29.6 to 36.4 per cent. As Beik writes, 'The Languedocian tax system was, above all, a sharing out of resources between king and notables'. Unpublished research on Languedocian finances in the 1780s reveals the same system at work a century later. Older works on Brittany and municipal finances suggest that the pattern was very probably a general one. In the *pays d'élection* the elites probably acquired a rather smaller share in the form of gratifications and administrative charges. All this evidence shows that the political system of the ancien régime was not a simple relationship between central government and periphery but was a complex interrelationship of mutual benefit to king, court and the regional elites. Only the 20 million poor gained little from it all.

If historians are correct to identify the exploitation of ceremony, patronage and clientage as an essential stage in the development and smooth functioning of the political system, then we must turn to another neglected feature of the ancien régime in order to complete the picture. The study of one institution helps us to understand the link between the administrative and social aspects of power: the royal court. In spite of numerous assertions to the contrary, the court was emphatically not simply a place where Louis XIII and Louis XIV domesticated the higher nobility, tamed it and turned it into a useless ornament. That was the case with many nobles, but the court was also the centre of power, the nerve-centre of the realm. This was true even when the court was still itinerant during the sixteenth century, and even more so when Louis XIV settled it at Versailles in 1682. The administration was housed in a wing of Versailles and every minister, councillor or secretary was also a courtier. That is to say that the administrators and bureaucrats were competing with other courtiers in an hierarchical environment well suited to the higher nobility. At court the king dispensed favours and held councils, both being vital aspects of government.

The advantages of the court system must first be explained, and then it will be possible to discuss some of the disadvantages it possessed as a political structure. First of all, the court was the only central institution of France, except for the council of state – which met at court. Given the legal impossibility of centralizing France because of provincial privileges, the court formed a vital link between centre and periphery. The court was the royal household and a proliferation of household offices existed with which to gratify aspirations to favour. The more important offices were not necessarily those with obvious political powers, but those which conferred easy access to the ear of the sovereign. That enabled a high aristocrat to obtain graces and favours for himself, his family and his clients, and thus preserve his prestige and extend his influence. For the king was the ultimate source of all patronage in the realm, at least in theory. He was at the pinnacle of the system, and the more important rewards were his for the granting. This being so, a wise ruler could achieve a balance between competing groups, and employ a policy of divide and rule to his own advantage or that of the state.

The greatest problem inherent in the court system was that it was the arena for competing factions. The existence of faction was no doubt the product of a mentality that viewed the interests of the aristocratic house, combined with its network of clients, as all-important. Powerful houses built up pressure groups and fought for advancement and further prestige. The in-fighting between factions could be very ruthless. They employed spies and pamphleteers to discover information about rivals and then blackened their reputation and attempted to discredit them. Factions were not above using their clientage networks to pull strings in local institutions in order to ensure the failure of the policies of rival groups. Thus, they could create political crises by their factional control of institutions. There are many examples of this right up to the 1780s, and we must regard it as the harmful side of a potentially useful system.

An important point about factions is that in a court society one group is never completely *out*, another never completely *in*. The court was really dominated by networks established by the grandest families of the realm – and often not just of the realm but of the international aristocracy. For example, the Rohan Guémenée were foreign princes resident in France, and could not be slighted whatever they did. In times of royal minorities these groups were especially dangerous, as rival families would manoeuvre for power in a less-restrained way. It was extremely difficult for a regent or a minister to build up a royal faction then, because of uncertainty about whether he would remain in favour in later years. This was particularly true of Mazarin.

Another serious problem, but one less remarked upon by historians, is the political conservatism which resulted from the balance between factions. To prove this it would be necessary to discuss the fate of reform policies in detail, which is impossible here. One example will serve to explain the problem. In the 1720s there was a reforming policy inaugurated by financiers, under the inexpert but enthusiastic first minister who was also a prince of the blood, which might have been of considerable benefit to the state. For various reasons he became unpopular by 1726 and was vanquished by factional intrigue. He was replaced by Fleury, soon to be both a cardinal and chief minister. During the next two years the cardinal constituted his own group of ministers and established his grip on policy, but the faction supporting him mistakenly regarded him as a pliable tool for its own interests, open to manipulation. He was astute enough to jump out of their pockets, but only at the cost of placating opposition and giving up all the reforms, which the faction had made political capital out of attacking and which had, in many cases, affected their interests adversely. Thus, the reforms which would have been of benefit to the state were abandoned as the price of staying in power. This is one example of many during the seventeenth and eighteenth centuries of the way in which the politics of balance became of necessity a politics of immobility. The balance of factions or parties dominated by self-interest was to create a similar political result during the Third Republic, much later.

Another feature is that factions were not so much in the hands of ministers, as ministers in the hands of factions. Ministerial initiatives were thus seriously limited by services owed to supporters and patrons. In this situation, the ruler was not in fact free to choose his ministers, he could only have candidates brought to his attention. Sometimes he was in difficulties for want of suitable candidates, with the result that many of those chosen were incompetent. And finally, in this social and political world, only a few devoted royal servants were interested in policy for its own sake. Most were preoccupied with the interests of family and clients, and with maintaining their position and prestige. Constant attention was paid to signs of favour or disfavour, with the result that adventurous policies, or reformist policies, were rarely initiated.

By the late eighteenth century France existed. The centrifugal forces were no longer strong enough to threaten disintegration of the state. They were managed by various techniques of control – bureaucracy, patronage, bluff, negotiation, propaganda – all centred upon a royal court. But the existence of numerous local power structures, liberties, privileges and legal variations, buttressed in some areas by irreducible centres of power such as parlements and estates, profoundly conditioned the state and limited its ability to develop and reform itself. It was a political system in a delicate balance of tensions, centripetal and centrifugal forces, centred upon a monarchy which gave state and society its ultimate rationale. Yet the monarchy had neither the theoretical nor the practical power to overcome the inevitable resistance of legally enshrined vested interests in order to reform itself. The only real initiative lay with the ministry, yet everything conspired to doom to failure the decisive exercise of initiative. In 1776 the reforming minister Turgot analysed the problem in his *Memoir on the municipalities*. As later events were to show, he was not alone in thinking that France had no constitution. In what sounds like a direct challenge to orthodox historians he wrote:

> The cause of the evil, Sire, comes from the fact that your nation has no *constitution*. It is a society composed of different orders badly united and of a people whose members have very few ties with one another; in which, consequently, each person is concerned by his own exclusive, private interests; and in which hardly anyone troubles to fulfil his duties nor to know his proper relationship to others; such that, in this perpetual war of claims and pretensions which reason and mutual enlightenment have never regulated, His Majesty is obliged to decide everything by himself or by his agents.

Twenty years later, royal initiatives at fiscal reform were to precipitate a crisis in the state which brought the whole edifice crashing down.

4　The End of the Ancien Régime

From the perspective of the Revolution and the sociologically influenced history of the twentieth century, it has been argued variously that the crisis of the 1780s was both social and political. The consensus is that there was a new mood and some increasingly visible changes in social and economic relations from the 1750s. Many still believe that the Revolution was caused by the political emergence of a rising class of capitalist bourgeoisie. The idea of an aristocratic or seigneurial reaction still has many adherents. Such oversimplified notions have been severely attacked since the 1950s but no new consensus has yet emerged. Recently, there has been a swing by some historians towards emphasizing the validity of more directly political explanations, without, however, denying the links between society and politics. This has not simplified the debate but it has at least led to greater sophistication and subtlety of explanation.

Before examining the crisis in detail it is as well to clarify the issues. The knowledge that the events of 1789 precipitated the world's first great modern revolution might lead to confusion, as hindsight prompts inappropriate questions. Above all, it prompts an emphasis upon the new, the apparently 'revolutionary', elements in society to explain 1789. The accent may be put upon the radical theories of the Enlightenment; or a seigneurial reaction postulated which, if one agrees with a rather mechanistic economic explanation of motivation, could explain peasant unrest in 1789. In fact, there are two, admittedly not wholly separate, issues to analyse. The first is the collapse of the ancien régime, the second is the Revolution, and they are far from identical in their causes. Unfortunately, they are often confused in historical debate on the assumption that the subsequent course of the upheaval is somehow inherent in the events of 1787–9. Part of the problem stems from the lack of a precise definition of the Revolution. Its extraordinary complexity defies simplification, and all the general theories of revolution have been influenced by the historiography of this one, which is rife with disagreements. One theory, for example that of the 'J-curve', makes much of a supposed credibility gap created by the disappointment of rising expectations during a sudden downturn in the previously expanding economy. This theory could not have existed before Labrousse's work on the movement of prices during the eighteenth century in which just

71

such a rise and fall in the economy is proved, unless the argument merely means to say no more than that the bad harvest in 1788 produced dissatisfaction. As yet no theory, Marxist or sociological, can explain a necessary relationship between peasant revolts and bourgeois/aristocratic aspirations for a constitution. Certainly, there was an historical connection between the two, but it was because of a fortuitous conjunction of bad weather and fiscal reform. To prove a necessary connection would require a far subtler and all-embracing theory than we yet have. The serious historian distrusts all theories until they are proved correct, even though he or she might find them stimulating in posing new questions.

To argue, like Edmund Burke, that developments subsequent to 1789 were all inherent in the ideas and events of that summer is therefore to devalue the history of France from 1789 to 1795. The anarchic course of the Revolution was not entirely predictable. A serious political crisis creates possibilities for action, in the surprise of an unexpected situation, which take the participants far off their intended course. A power struggle in which several groups, moderate and radical, are attempting to impose their aims leads to the whole situation becoming subject to twists and turns of fate unpredicted by the actors. Radical solutions which could only be envisaged by the most extreme thinkers are sometimes adopted as the complexity of the political situation makes them more acceptable. The prospects for the success of radicals in May 1789 seemed slim; it was the inactivity of the ministry that provided them with their opportunity in June. In many respects the revolutionary situation created the culture and ideology of what was to become the Great Revolution. That revolutionary situation was created by the collapse of the old régime.

Over the last two decades the orthodox interpretation of the Revolution has not fared well. Marxist historians have become far more subtle than they were a generation ago, but still believe that the Revolution was intrinsically the political manifestation of the development of capitalism in society, against the nobility and in the interests of the bourgeoisie. New conclusions on both these groups have been presented in Chapter 1, and they tend to undermine this view. No one denies that the Revolution was largely the work of a bourgeoisie, but it remains to be seen what sort of bourgeoisie. Cobban pointed out that most revolutionaries were venal office-holders and lawyers and very few were 'capitalists' of any sort. From an investigation of types of capitalism in the eighteenth century, Taylor concluded that a capitalist bourgeoisie in the Marxist (nineteenth-century) sense existed only in small numbers and that the predominant form of capitalist wealth was proprietary. Hence any connection between the Revolution and nineteenth-century industrial or commercial capitalism seems difficult to accept. Bourgeois aspirations remained traditional: even in the 1780s, the 'typical' bourgeois was a *rentier* aiming at a noble life-style unsullied by sordid commercialism. The rising price of ennobling and venal offices is a reflection of their aspirations. Little is left, therefore, of the orthodox theory to convince us of a revolution whose origins lay with a class of rising capitalists. However, it may be that later stages of the revolutionary process witnessed the emergence of other groups or sets of motives such as those of the commercial classes and the artisans. Interests were as complex as the social structure of the ancien régime, whose institutions tended to mask fine differences of social class in our modern sense of the term. Thus, the notion of class struggle must not be ruled out in the 1790s.

It is more difficult to assess the fall-back position of some Marxists, namely that in effect the Revolution was capitalist because it advanced the cause of capitalism both by ending privileged impediments to trade and by opening careers to talents. In fact, this argument can only be evaluated in the light of an answer to the question of whether or not the natural progress of trade would have led to the abandoning of impediments at a later date and more peacefully, as in Germany in the 1830s. Objectively, the Revolution may have been capitalist in this sense (but was it therefore historically necessary?) although very few of the participants in the legislative processes seem to have been identifiable with such interests. Again we witness the temptation to deduce motives from results, and to use the events of the period to validate a determinist view of history in which there is no apparent connection between so-called objective forces and the conscious aims of the actors.

As we have seen, it is usual to regard the Enlightenment as the fountainhead of the ideas which formed the intellectual origins of the Revolution. Concepts of national sovereignty and the constitution are associated with Rousseau and Montesquieu, and these are key concepts during the Revolution, as is the idea of progress. In assessing this argument it is well to remember three points. First, that the end of the old régime was not synonymous with the origins of the Revolution. Second, that the revolutionary mentality was not simply an extension of the doctrines invoked from 1787 to 1789; what we might call a paradigmatic shift occurred in 1789, as the terms of the debate altered under the impact of events: the old political mould was broken and a new one was cast. The ideas and language of the Enlightenment were important in the work of reconstruction and in the ideological debates that took place during the later Revolution, and above all they were important as a justification for courses of action deemed necessary by the revolutionaries; they were of much less significance in the development of a revolutionary situation before 1789. Third, when dealing with the impact of ideas upon events, we should remind ourselves that it is not so much the idea itself or the intentions of the author which is significant, but the context in which it is used and the purpose to which it is put. The ideas of Mably and Rousseau were appealed to by both revolutionaries and counter-revolutionaries.

It should be clear from the account of the last years of the régime, which concludes this chapter, that many of the concepts motivating the actors in the final drama of the ancien régime did not have their roots

73

in the Englightenment, even if their language sometimes concealed this. Only after the autumn of 1788 did radical Enlightened ideas become more general in pamphlets, and these had their main practical impact when the form of politics and debate had been transformed in 1789.

In the ancien régime, political debate was not principally theoretical in nature: disputes were about privileges and rights, and the usual form of discussion was to cull arguments from suitable texts and cobble together an argument from authority, as a buttress to more practical claims. For example, the concept of national sovereignty was not yet employed to advocate a republic, and there were almost no republicans in France until 1791, well into the revolutionary period. According to Montesquieu and Rousseau, France was too large and populous a state for a democratic form of government. In the 1780s, the appeal to the nation was an attempt to justify privileged resistance to innovations brought about by the ministry, and was designed to protect jurisdiction, rights and liberties against encroachment. In so far as this was a traditional protest against use of the royal prerogative, it was a question of old wine in new bottles, for the idea of national sovereignty had been exploited in the sixteenth century by both Protestants and Catholics.

The notion of a constitution was not derived simply from John Locke or the Enlightenment, but had deeper French roots and quite a different pedigree. It was neither bourgeois nor especially aristocratic (though more the latter), but owed a great deal of its development to the religious disputes of the eighteenth century. The word 'constitution' changed its meaning during that century – early on it appears to have meant no more than the way the state was made up, but finally, and quite when is not yet clear, it came to mean a set of prescriptive rules and regulations defining the various powers of the body politic. Interestingly enough, a crucial stage in the evolution, transition and development of the idea was reached during the quarrel over the enforcement of the Bull *Unigenitus*, which condemned Jansenism in 1713, involving the crown, the parlements and the recalcitrant Jansenists from 1730 to 1762. Believing themselves to be unjustly, and therefore despotically, oppressed, the Jansenists revived and turned to their advantage theories of despotism and the legal limitations on royal power, making the parlement of Paris their champion (Campbell, 1985 and Van Kley, 1984). A large pamphlet literature gave these ideas a wider currency and set the terms of the debate from 1771 onwards.

It was principally in the context of a struggle for provincial privileges and legal rights against despotism in the form of new taxation, that the American War of Independence was interpreted by Frenchmen. The American struggle was greeted with sympathy in France because it was seen not as the emergence of modern bourgeois democracy but as the triumph of worthy provincial aristocrats and landowners over British tyranny and sordid commercialism. A Breton, a Provençal or a Dauphinois could identify with these traditional values during the debate over administrative centralization and the reorganization of taxation which began in 1787. None of these ideas was yet associated with a revolutionary future and all were employed in the age-old debate over the just limits of royal power in the ancien régime.

Instead of explaining the crisis of 1787–9 in the light of the subsequent revolution, it is therefore more appropriate to set it in the long-term context of the old order. So many of its separate constituent elements are typical of the procedures and structures of the régime that one almost wonders why it did not happen earlier. As early as the 1750s and 1760s the Marquis d'Argenson and the philosopher Mably predicted, on the strength of their observations of politics, a major political crisis involving finance and the Paris parlement. A long perspective helps us to avoid such obvious errors as regarding the nobility's defence of its privileges in 1787 as an aggressive 'noble reaction' dating from earlier in the century (Doyle, 1972). The fact is that nobles had never been effectively excluded from power even under Louis XIV and there was no need for an offensive to regain lost influence. Nor was the fiscal problem a new one. The state had tottered from one financial crisis to another since the Hundred Years War and had never succeeded in effecting adequate reform. Successive attempts at reform and the survival of devious fiscal practices had left a legacy of suspicion of governmental motives shared by all groups in society. Consequently, an antiquated system of unfairly assessed taxes, fiscal immunities, private financial offices and an inadequate credit system survived into an age when the everyday expenses of government normally required a large revenue, and the costs of war pushed the system beyond its limits.

The ancien régime was a social and political system which, like all régimes, contained many tensions. Conflicts between social groups, and particularly between institutions, could become especially dangerous in the traditionally minded society governed by precedent but not controlled by a clear constitutional framework. What to us appear minor issues of precedence and jurisdiction could, in the absence of forums for a political dialogue and in a system in which possession was nine-tenths of the law, escalate into major disputes raising 'constitutional' issues. Numerous crises rehearsed the pattern of claim and counter-claim, until apparently irreconcilable conflict led to deadlock. There are examples at the time of the Fronde, during the reign of Louis XIV and, increasingly, during the eighteenth century, involving the Paris and provincial parlements. In each case the outcome depended upon ministerial pressure, covert negotiations and the specific political circumstances. A weak ministry might capitulate, or succumb to factional intrigue; a strong one would generally dupe the opposition with a show of force and then offer a face-saving compromise. It was always a delicate balancing act, however, because honour had to be maintained and the question of the limits to monarchical authority was best left vague. A show of force would lead, as in the 1760s and the *coup d'état* of 1771, to accusations of despotism.

It must be emphasized that such conflicts were a part of the very structure of the régime. From this perspective it is perhaps surprising that the régime survived for so long before an insurmountable crisis led to a questioning of the fundamental structure and a tearing aside of the veil of myth which protected state power. Such a crisis occurred in the 1780s.

The ultimate fiscal crisis was precipitated by participation in the American War of Independence (1778–83) against Britain. Instead of financing the hostilities by increased taxation, enormous debts were incurred by the state under the controller-generalship of Jacques Necker, a Genevan banker who made his career in France. Necker and his two successors, Joly de Fleury and d'Ormesson, floated large government loans whose repayment was to create a deficit in the immediate future. After the end of the war it was increasingly difficult to meet the enormous expense of servicing the debt because the royal budget was in annual deficit. Charles-Alexandre de Calonne, an ambitious former intendant, became controller general in November 1783 and had no option but to raise further loans. His policy was to conceal the financial state of the realm and increase public confidence by, on the one hand, the old policy of prompt payment of interest, and on the other, by a liberal policy of freer trade, inducements to manufacturers, and public works intended to develop the economy in the long term. To keep himself in favour he permitted more extravagant spending at court and paid off the debts of the king's influential brothers. This was a policy which may have been politically necessary but which redounded to his discredit with Neckerite critics, who portrayed him as prodigal and irresponsible. In the present state of studies, the question of whether Calonne was a sincere reformer or something of an adventurer remains a mystery. Critics have pointed out that he waited until August 1786, when the financial situation was becoming quite desperate and royal bankruptcy foreseeable, before attacking the formidable problem of taxation. From this time until the collapse of the régime the spectre of a 'hideous bankruptcy' haunted the ministry. The need to maintain public confidence, and the confidence of investors at home and in the money markets abroad, in order to fill the all too necessary state loans, seriously limited the ministry's room for manoeuvre. It was the credit crisis which eventually forced the capitulation to demands for a national body whose consent was required for peacetime taxation and reform: the dangerous expedient of the Estates General.

Normally, loans were registered in the Paris parlement, but from 1785 strong opposition could be expected. Its first president and chief rapporteur, duty-bound to defend the king's interests, were involved in factional intrigue and were implacably opposed to Calonne. They were quite prepared to neglect their duty to the crown and even pull strings to make registration unlikely. Yet without free legal registration in the courts investors would have no confidence in the terms of the loan. Calonne had his back to the wall. He therefore decided upon a wide-ranging reform plan (largely derived from an old memoir by Turgot) to be presented to an Assembly of Notables early in 1787. He hoped that with the support of a quasi-national body he could later force the plans through the courts at a *lit de justice*. As far as reform was concerned, his problem was a simple one: how to arrange a permanently increased royal revenue without further imposing on the poor who were already overburdened. The solution was equally straightforward in theory: the orders and communities enjoying exemptions must pay their fair share of taxation. Vauban had diagnosed the problem and proposed proportional land taxation as early as 1707, but neither Louis XIV then, nor the Pâris brothers in 1725, nor Machault in 1749 had managed to enact such legislation successfully. Calonne's plans of 1787 proposed ending all fiscal privileges and taxing land according to its leasable value. In essence, the administrative reforms – the creation of parish and provincial assemblies – were all designed to facilitate the levying of this tax without alienating too much executive authority. With such a far-reaching set of reforms would Calonne be any more successful than his predecessors?

The Assembly of Notables met on 22 February 1787, a week after the death of Vergennes, Calonne's chief supporter in the royal council. Numbering 144, the notables included many of the most prominent individuals in the realm. There were princes of the blood and peers, archbishops and leading parlementaires but also twenty-five mayors of towns from the Third Estate. Nevertheless, the Assembly represented the views of the privileged to an overwhelming extent, while few of Calonne's presumed supporters actually remained loyal. Opposition to the reform plans was fierce. Calonne refused to disclose the extent of the debt and thus gave the impression that the Assembly was intended to rubber-stamp his plans. Inept management, offended dignity, factional intrigue from the ambitious Loménie de Brienne and the Neckerites, all these factors ensured the dismissal of Calonne in April 1787, discredited and unsuccessful. It is noteworthy that criticisms of his plans employed traditional arguments, although they were sometimes dressed up in the fashionable constitutional language. Many notables feigned acceptance of fiscal equality in principle but argued that it was actually unconstitutional. Their main thrust was reserved for the proposed provincial assemblies against which feeling was strong and whose organization was easy to attack. With voting by head rather than order and a mixing of the social ranks they were an affront to notions of privilege. Not only did they represent an attack on the natural leaders of society but also a significant increase in royal 'despotism', because the royal intendant was to have an important role in them. As Le Blanc de Castillon said in debate, 'The people should be separated from the upper orders by the reservation of dignity and power to the latter. The proposed plan has two defects: that of having exaggerated the popular element in the parish assemblies; and that of giving the intendant too great an authority in the provincial assemblies: Republicanism and Despotism' (Hardman, p. 36).

As Goodwin has shown, it was a clever tactic because without the assemblies the taxes would be unworkable and thus the whole project would founder. Archbishop Loménie de Brienne succeeded Calonne in May and presented modified plans which were only partly acceptable. The Assembly was therefore disbanded, but in the summer the Paris parlement felt strong enough to refuse the fiscal plans on the grounds that the Estates General alone were competent to enact non-specific peacetime taxation. There began an old-style parlementaire crisis with its cycle of remonstrances and exiles, but this time the government was weak and everyone knew it. On October 17 the agronomist Arthur Young dined in Paris:

> One opinion pervaded the whole company, that they are on the eve of some great revolution (i.e. change) in the government: that every thing points to it: the confusion in the finances great; with a deficit impossible to provide for without the states-general of the kingdom, yet no ideas formed of what would be the consequence of their meeting: no minister existing, or to be looked to in or out of power, with such decisive talents as to promise any other remedy than palliative ones: a prince on the throne, with excellent dispositions, but without the resources of a mind that could govern in such a moment without ministers: a court buried in pleasure and dissipation; and adding to the distress, instead of endeavouring to be placed in a more independent situation: a great ferment amongst all ranks of men, who are eager for some change, without knowing what to look to, or to hope for: and a strong leaven of liberty, increasing every hour since the American revolution; altogether form a combination of circumstances that promise e'er long to ferment into motion, if some master of hand, of very superior talents, and inflexible courage, is not found at the helm to guide events, instead of being driven by them. It is very remarkable, that such conversation never occurs, but a bankruptcy is a topic: the curious question on which is, would a bankruptcy occasion a civil war, and a total overthrow of the government?

In November 1787 the king finally registered a massive five-year loan in the parlement and agreed to the calling of the Estates General in 1792. Parlementaire opposition continued and this led Brienne to attempt another coup in the manner of Maupeou in 1771. By the May Edicts of 1788 the parlements had their functions severely limited and in future royal edicts were to be registered by a plenary court of judges appointed by the crown. The promulgation of these 'despotic' edicts in the provinces was the signal for what historians term the 'revolt of the notables'. The reaction was particularly violent in Brittany, with its tradition of liberties, and Dauphiné where the lead was taken by a revived provincial assembly. The British ambassador recorded that 'In Dauphiné and other Provinces no taxes whatever can be collected, and accounts of some fresh act of revolt and disobedience arrive every day from different parts of the

Kingdom'. In retrospect, the provincial nobility was too successful for its own good. At first united with the Third Estate against what was universally perceived as royal 'despotism', its insistence upon aristocratic privileges in provincial assemblies ended by antagonizing and disillusioning the bourgeoisie. This was a general quarrel between orders rather than classes, and in some provinces there was violence by early 1789.

By August 1788 the state was on the verge of bankruptcy. Brienne was dismissed and Necker, creditworthy and with the carefully nurtured reputation of being a financial wizard, was brought back this time as chief minister. His policy was to increase the creditworthiness of the government by bowing before the storm: he reinstated the parlements and advanced the date of the meeting of the Estates General to 1 January 1789. Unfortunately, the Paris parlement failed to show either gratitude or repentance, nor any political wisdom. Its first act was to decree that the Estates General should meet according to the forms of its last meeting in 1614, although in previous sittings the form had varied. This was an open challenge to the newly awakened Third Estate, who realized that greater fiscal and social equality depended upon a doubling of the numbers of the Third and voting by head not by order. Although Necker could see that a royal alliance with the Third would be expedient, he lacked the strength in the council, where blindness and intrigue still reigned, to impose his will. Right up until June 1789 the traditionalist aristocratic opposition, which was influential especially at court, could not perceive the extent to which power to resist reform had slipped from their hands. They behaved as if the new force of public opinion could be resisted and politics carried on in the old, underhand, courtly fashion. Necker was able to insist upon double representation for the Third Estate, but the question of voting was left fatefully unresolved.

France was now in political ferment, and had been since the summer of 1788, after the troubles and when effective freedom of the press had been granted in preparation for the Estates General. Of the 2500 or so pamphlets published before May 1789 the one which is most celebrated is *What is the Third Estate?* by the Abbé Siéyès. It helped to define the terms of the debate and crystallize it around the issues of privilege and of the future role of the Third Estate. Political debate took place openly in cafés, on the promenades and in places where newsmongers gathered. In Paris the Palais Royal was a haven for all orators and polemicists. From January 1789, the electoral process must have politicized many who had never previously considered political change to be a serious possibility. The drawing up of lists of grievances, the *cahiers*, by all orders and parishes led to debate and expectations of change. Although this was just what conservatives feared, at this stage the hope was generally for moderate reform rather than radical change. According to a large sample of the *cahiers*, from the Third Estate 71 per cent of rural parish *cahiers* and 49 per cent of those of the upper urban corps did not express political grievances, if politics is defined as prescribing some governmental changes subsequently enacted (Taylor, 1972). The electoral process ensured that no peasants or workers were elected and so the deputies for the Third were overwhelmingly from the professional or upper bourgeoisie. These groups were obviously looking to the monarchy to lead them in the direction of fiscal reform and away from despotism. Since reform of taxation was clearly necessary, bourgeois property-owners were determined that the nobility should not be allowed to escape its fair share of the imposition; and the professional groups, especially the lawyers, were hoping for an opportunity to enter professions closed to them by privileges: they dreamt of emulating that new man, Cicero, in Republican Rome, where virtue was thought to have reigned. The peasants would have to make their grievances known by different methods.

When the Estates General assembled in Versailles on 5 May 1789, its 1201 deputies comprised 610 members of the Third Estate, some 291 nobles, of whom at least 50 may be counted liberal, and about 300 ecclesiastics, mostly parish *curés* who would side with the Third Estate. The next few weeks were of crucial importance for the breakdown of the régime and the emergence of a revolutionary situation. Far from giving the Estates a firm lead and imposing a solution, the ministry still left the vital issue of voting unresolved. It must have been clear to all the legally minded deputies, from commoner lawyers to aristocratic parlementaires, that the fate of privilege and the extent of fiscal reform depended upon the Third Estate outvoting the first two orders on these matters. Thus, voting by head and not by order was essential to reformers. Deadlock at once ensued when the Third refused to verify its elections unless the other orders assembled with it. Insistence upon this procedure was a clever tactic which would have led to an effective amalgamation and voting by head. The apparent intransigence of the first two estates over the next few weeks did much to undermine their credibility and led to a radicalization of the situation as deputies became exasperated. During these weeks of unsuccessful parleys and inactivity, clubs formed to discuss politics and prepare for the sessions, and in this the Breton deputies played a special part. After much hesitation, on 12 June the estate decided to verify the powers of all 1201 deputies, by roll call, and on 17 June the Third, joined by only a few of the privileged, declared itself the National Assembly. It claimed the right to give France a constitution (although what this meant remained vague). This forced the issue and the clergy voted by a narrow majority to join the Assembly. By now, the challenge to the monarchy was too strong to ignore; a royal session was prepared in which the king was to exert his authority. The closing of the hall in preparation of 20 June frightened the Assembly, and the momentous Tennis Court oath was taken, by which the deputies, fearing a coup, vowed not to separate until France had been given a constitution. When the royal session took place on 23 June, the moderate proposals from the court were simply too little and too late. Fear of the Parisian mob and the unreliability of the troops prompted a royal capitulation four days later, when the king ordered both the privileged orders to join the Third Estate. But the court was now reactionary and troops were called to the Versailles region to intimidate the Assembly. In Paris, unrest reached the gravest of proportions and the dismissal of Necker on 11 July provoked the final crisis. Riots broke out and on 14 July the search for arms to defend the Assembly led to the storming of the Bastille, a fortress dominating the city. The fall of the Bastille is the symbolic event marking the end of the ancien régime. It sent a shock wave through French society which generated further rural disorders and municipal revolutions.

The victory of the Assembly was made possible by the widespread disorders which seized France in the spring and summer of 1789. These were not of political origin, although vague hopes of reform and rumours played a part, but were primarily caused by the economic crisis. The grain harvest of 1788 had been disastrous and the price of bread for a family rose by the spring of 1789 from half an artisan's daily wage to nearly nine-tenths of it. As always, the repercussions of high expenditure on bread were a decline in spending on other goods, especially textiles, and this created both rural and urban unemployment and only worsened the subsistence crisis. During the spring, *taxations populaires* and food riots became increasingly frequent. In April the tension in Paris led to large-scale riots, fuelled by rumours of wage cuts, in which the Réveillon manufacture was attacked. By July, orators such as Camille Desmoulins were spreading rumours and dosing the climate of economic insecurity with political opinions. The police force was quite inadequate to cope with such widespread distress and disorder, and troops were reluctant to fire on compatriots.

In the countryside, economic insecurity, the awakening hopes of reform, fears of brigands and aristocratic malevolence produced the Great Fear of late July and early August. This, more than any bourgeois revolution, was to bring about the end of the feudal system of seigneurial dues. Waves of fear and disorder, beginning in several epicentres and spreading by rumour, led to peasant attacks in some areas on rural châteaux and the burning of manorial records and title deeds to feudal dues. Rural France was in anarchy and bourgeois fears for property were aroused by the violence. There was a need to preserve order and defend the political victory. Urban militias were formed to repress peasant outbreaks and a municipal revolution occurred in numerous towns, echoing the one in Paris. Oligarchical town councils fell from power or were forced to compromise with bourgeois interests (Ligou, 1960). Politicians in Versailles were well aware that their victory over the court and the privileged orders owed a great deal to the disorders, but feared greatly for their own property. This situation produced as a legislative response the dismantling of the old régime in recognition of the fait accompli by the peasants.

The extraordinary episode of the night of 4 August 1789 witnessed a frenzy of self-denial by deputies anxious to preserve order at the price of sacrificing their own and others' privileges. Judged inevitable, the sacrifice was prepared in advance and begun by liberal nobles who, in fact, had little to lose. Venality of office, seigneurial rights, corporations and all forms of privilege were voted away by acclamation until three in the morning. But on 5 August, cooler heads reflected on the sacrifice and the final decrees of 11 August attempted to limit the losses. Compensation was voted for offices, and, where possible, distinctions were drawn between useful (that is, profitable) rights and honorific ones, only the latter being freely abandoned. Nevertheless, the damage had been done and later years of revolution were to ensure the final destruction of the seigneurial régime and privileges. The Declaration of the Rights of Man and the Duties of the Citizen of 26 August was to establish the philosophical basis of a new political system and a different social order. The political agencies of the ancien régime had simply ceased to function during the summer of revolution.

Historians on the Right, with an idealized view of the régime, have perhaps found it convenient to agree with an explanation which puts the accent upon changes and rising tensions from the 1750s. Such a view tends to conceal the permanent tension in state and society and the exploitation inherent in the economic system at an earlier period. Marxists have argued against this in their analysis of the régime, unfortunately after characterizing it, misleadingly, as 'feudal'. Their own account of the final decades of the régime has been marred both by a doctrinaire insistence on the 'bourgeois' nature of revolution and by the distortions produced by historical determinism and hindsight. Making use of a longer perspective and concentrating upon the structures, it is now possible to show that the social and economic tensions which were undoubtedly present in 1789 were more typical of the ancien régime than has often been thought. Certainly, the political crisis which brought them to the surface was entirely in the vein of previous disputes between institutions, estates and factions, and employed traditional methods of political conduct. Only during the Revolution itself did new vistas open up for political action, and it then became possible to exploit the concepts and language of politics in a new way.

Perhaps an interpretation which fails to give the Enlightenment and imminent social transformation a central place will find many critics. But if it should lead to reflection and the posing of new questions, or put the accent upon fresh answers to some older ones, then it will have achieved its aim. What was the meaning of 'liberty' and 'constitution', concepts of which so much was made? How did members of the professional bourgeoisie, especially lawyers, view state and society in the 1780s; and what was the role of the merchant class, so little represented in the National Assembly? Historians are already searching for answers to questions such as these; their answers may be expected to modify our views still further.

Epilogue

The ancien régime in France was a unique combination of economic, social, political and ideological elements, not static but nevertheless retaining coherence over a long period. What happened in the summer of 1789 was the collapse of the edifice and the end of this specific conjunction of features. Most importantly, absolute monarchy, hierarchy, order and corporatism ceased to rule society. Henceforth, it would be impossible to recreate the shattered myths and the consensus which had held politics and society together as a régime. The Revolution produced ideological debate and the chasm between Left and Right which still characterizes politics today, and one of the elements of this division is the view held of the ancien régime itself. And yet, many of the individual components of the régime survived long into the nineteenth century or are indeed still with us. Administratively, the new French state adopted many of the pre-revolutionary structures, but imbued them with a different ethic. A powerful ideological nostalgia survives for a mythical ancien régime. Economically, historians speak of an economic system of old-régime type at least until 1848 in France. Socially, perhaps the Revolution merely recognized what was already almost a fact, namely that French society was ruled by an elite of notables to which access was largely controlled by wealth and life-style. However the régime is assessed, interpretations will vary. No specialist on the ancien régime or the Revolution would deny that the debate remains open. Therein lies a good part of its fascination.

References

Antoine, M. 1970: *Le Conseil du Roi sous le règne de Louis XV*, Paris and Geneva.

Asher, E.L. 1960: *The Resistance to the Maritime Classes: the survival of feudalism in the France of Colbert*, Berkeley, California.

Beik, W. 1985: *Absolutism and society in seventeenth-century France: state power and provincial aristocracies in Languedoc*, Cambridge.

Bodin, J. (1576) 1962: *The six books of a commonweale*, (ed.), K.D. McRae, facsimile reprint of 1601 translation, Cambridge, Massachusetts.

Bonney, R. 1981: *The king's debts: finance and politics in France, 1589–1661*, Oxford.

Bouchard, G. 1972: *Le village immobile: Sennely-en-Sologne au XVIIIe siècle*, Paris.

Campbell, P.R. 1985: 'The conduct of politics in France in the time of the cardinal de Fleury, 1723–1743', PhD thesis, University of London.

Castan, Y. 1974: *Honnêteté et relations sociales en Languedoc, 1715–1780*. Paris.

Darnton, R. 1984: *The great cat massacre and other episodes in French cultural history*, London.

Delumeau, J. 1977: *Catholicism between Luther and Voltaire*, Paris.

Dessert, D. 1976: 'Pouvoir et finance au XVIIe siècle: la fortune de Mazarin', *Revue d'Histoire moderne et contemporaine*, XXXIII.

Dessert, D. 1984: *Argent, pouvoir et société au Grand siècle*, Paris.

Dessert, D. and Journet, J.L. 1975 'Le lobby Colbert: un royaume ou une affaire de famille?' *Annales: E.S.C.* XXX.

Doyle, W. 1972: 'Was there an aristocratic reaction in pre-revolutionary France?' *Past and present*, LVII.

Du Bouëtzies de Kergouen, A. 1875: *Recherches sur les états de Bretagne: la tenue de 1736*, Paris.

Du Fail, N. 1928: *Propos rustiques, suivis des Balivernies*, ed. L.R. Lefevre, Paris.

Duby, G. 1980: *The three orders. Feudal society imagined*, Chicago.

Dupâquier, J. 1979: *La population française au XVIIe et XVIIIe siècles*, Paris.

Durand, Y. (ed.) 1966: *Cahiers de doléances des paroisses du bailliage de Troyes*. Paris.

Emmanuelli, F.-X. 1981: *Un mythe de l'absolutisme bourbonien: l'intendance, du milieu du XVIIe siècle à la fin du XVIIIe siècle (France, Espagne, Amerique)*, Provence.

Febvre, L. 1982: *The problem of unbelief in the sixteenth century: the religion of Rabelais*, Cambridge, Massachusetts.

Ferrier-Caverivière, N. 1981: *L'image de Louis XIV dans la littérature française de 1660 à 1715*, Paris.

Giesey, R. 1960: *The royal funeral ceremony in Renaissance France*, Geneva.

Goodwin, A. 1946: 'Calonne, The Assembly of Notables and the origins of the révolte nobiliaire', *English Historical Review*, 61.

Guenée, B. (1964) 1972: 'The history of the state in France at the end of the Middle Ages...', in P.S. Lewis, (ed.) *The recovery of France in the fifteenth century*, London.

Guenée, B. and Lehoux, F. 1968: *Les entrées royales françaises de 1328 à 1515*, Paris.

Gutton, J.P. 1981: *Domestiques et serviteurs dans la France de l'ancien régime*, Paris.

Hamscher, A.N. 1976: *The parlement of Paris after the Fronde, 1653–1673*, Pittsburg.

Harding, R.R. 1978: *Anatomy of power elite: the provincial governors of early modern France*, London.

Hardman, J. (ed.) 1981: *The French revolution*, London.

Kettering, S. 1986: *Patrons, brokers and clients in seventeenth-century France*, New York.

Lefebvre, P. 1973: 'Aspects de la fidélité en France au XVIIe siècle: le cas des agents du prince de Condé', *Revue historique*.

Ligou, D. 1960: 'A propos de la révolution municipale', *Revue d'Histoire économique et sociale*.

Lottin, A. 1977: 'La qualité de la vie chez l'ouvrier de textile lillois', in 'La qualité de la vie au XVIIe siècle', a colloquium, *Marseille*, no. 109.

Mandrou, R. (1961), 1975: *Introduction to modern France, 1500–1640. An essay in historical psychology*, London.

Mettam, R. 1988: *Power and faction in Louis XIV's France*, Oxford.

Mousnier, R. and Hartung, F. 1955: 'Quelques problèmes concernant la monarchie absolue', in *Comitato internazionale di Scienze storiche, X Congresso internazionale, Roma, 1955*, Florence.

Pagès, G. 1932a: 'Essai sur l'évolution des institutions administratives en France...', *Revue d'Histoire moderne*, XII.

Pagès, G. 1932b: 'La vénalité des offices dans l'ancienne France', *Revue historique*, CLXIX.

Platter, T. 1963: *Journal of a younger brother. The life of Thomas Platter as a medical student in Montpellier...*, ed. and trans. by S. Jennett, Muller, London.

Ranum, O.A. 1963: *Richelieu and the councillors of Louis XIII*, Oxford.

Reinhard, M. 1956: 'Elite et noblesse dans la seconde moitié du XVIIIe siècle', *Revue d'Histoire moderne et contemporaine*, III.

Rétif de la Bretonne, N. 1986: *My Father's life*, R.G. Veasey (trans. of *La vie de mon père*), Gloucester.

Sée, H. 1927: *Economic and social conditions in France during the eighteenth century*, New York.

Seyssel, C. de (1515), 1981: *The monarchy of France*, New Haven, Connecticut.

Taylor, G.V. 1967: 'Non-capitalist wealth and the origins of the French Revolution', *American Historical Review*, LXX.

Taylor, G.V. 1972: 'Revolutionary and non-revolutionary content in the *cahiers* of 1789', *French Historical Studies*.

Thompson, E.P. 1971: 'The moral economy of the English crowd in the eighteenth century', *Past and Present*.

Van Kley, D. 1984: *The Damiens affair and the unravelling of the ancien régime, 1750–1770*, Princeton, New Jersey.

Vicens Vives, J. 1960: 'The administrative structure of the state in the sixteenth and seventeenth centuries', in H.J. Cohn (ed.), *Government in Reformation Europe, 1520–1560*, London.

Wood, J.B. 1980: *The nobility of the élection of Bayeux, 1463–1666*, Princeton, New Jersey.

XVIIᵉ siècle 1979: 'La mobilité sociale au XVIIᵉ siècle', *Dix-septième siècle*.

Guide to further reading

Baker, K.M. (ed.) *The old regime and the French Revolution*. Chicago and London, 1987.

Baker, K.M. (ed.) *The political culture of the Old Regime*. Oxford, 1987.

Beauroy, J. (ed.) *The wolf and the lamb: popular culture in France from the old regime to the nineteenth century*. Santiago, 1977.

Bergin, J. *Cardinal Richelieu: power and the pursuit of wealth*. New Haven, Connecticut, 1985.

Bloch, M. *French rural history: an essay on its basic characteristics*. London, 1966.

Bloch, M. *The royal touch: sacred monarchy and scrofula in England and France*. London, 1973.

Braudel, F. *Civilisation and capitalism 15th–18th century*. 3 vols. London, 1981–4.

Briggs, R. *Early modern France*. Oxford, 1977.

Burke, P. *Popular culture in early modern Europe*. London, 1978.

Church, W.F. *Louis XIV in historical thought*. New York, 1976.

Cobban, A. *The social interpretation of the French Revolution*. London, 1964.

Cobban, A. *Aspects of the French Revolution*. London, 1968.

Coveney, P.J. (ed.) *France in crisis, 1620–1675*. London, 1977.

Dakin, D. *Turgot and the ancien régime in France*. London, 1939.

Davis, N.Z. *Society and culture in early modern France: eight essays*. London, 1975.

Dewald, J. *The formation of a provincial nobility*. Princeton, New Jersey, 1980.

Durand, Y. (ed.) *Cahiers de doléances des paroisses du bailliage de Troyes...* Paris, 1966.

Durand, Y. (ed.) *Hommage à Roland Mousnier: clientèles et fidélités en Europe à l'époque moderne*. Paris, 1981.

Egret, J. *The French pre-revolution, 1787–1789*. Chicago, 1977.

Furet, F. and Ozouf, J. *Reading and writing*. Cambridge, 1982.

Gerhard, D. *Old Europe, A study in continuity 1000–1800*. 1981.

Goubert, P. *The ancien régime, vol. 1: French society 1600–1750*. London, 1973.

Gutton, J.-P. *La sociabilité villageoise dans l'ancienne France*. Paris, 1979.

Hanley, S. *The lit de justice of the kings of France: a constitutional ideology in legend, ritual and discourse*. Princeton, New Jersey, 1983.

Hatton, R. (ed.) *Louis XIV and absolutism.* London, 1976.

Hufton, O. *The poor in eighteenth-century France, 1750–1789.* Oxford, 1974.

Huizinga, J. *The waning of the middle ages.* London, 1955.

Jackson, R.A. *Vive le roi! A history of the French coronation from Charles V to Charles X.* Chapel Hill, North Carolina, 1984.

Kierstead, R.F. (ed.) *State and society in seventeenth-century France.* New York, 1975.

Labrousse, C.E. *Esquisse du mouvement des prix et des revenus en France au XVIIIe siècle.* 2 vols, Paris, 1933.

Le Roy Ladurie, E. *The territory of the historian.* Brighton, 1979.

Le Roy Ladurie, E. *The mind and method of the historian.* Brighton, 1981.

Le Roy Ladurie, E. *The French peasantry 1450–1660.* Aldershot, 1987.

Lefebvre, G. *The coming of the French Revolution.* Princeton, New Jersey, 1947.

Lewis, P.S. *Later medieval France: the polity.* London, 1968.

Lewis, P.S. (ed.) *The recovery of France in the fifteenth century.* New York, 1972.

Major, J.R. 'The crown and the aristocracy in renaissance France', *American Historical Review,* LXXIX, 1964.

Major, J.R. *Representative government in early modern France.* New Haven, Connecticut, 1980.

Mandrou, R. *De la culture populaire au XVIIe et XVIIIe siècles,* Paris, 1964.

Mandrou, R. *From humanism to science, 1400–1700.* London, 1979.

Mettam, R. (ed.) *Government and society in Louis XIV's France.* London, 1977.

Meuvret, J. *Etudes d'histoire économique.* Paris, 1971.

Mousnier, R. *Peasant uprisings in seventeenth-century France, Russia and China.* London, 1971.

Muchembled, R. (ed.) *La sorcière au village (XV-XVIIIe siècle).* Paris, 1979.

Pagès, G. *La monarchie d'ancien régime en France.* Paris, 1928.

Richet, D. *La France moderne: l'esprit des institutions.* Paris, 1973.

Roche, D. *The people of Paris: an essay in popular culture in the eighteenth century.* Leamington Spa, 1987.

Rothkrug, L. *Opposition to Louis XIV.* Princeton, 1965.

Rothney, J. *The Brittany affair and the crisis of the ancien régime.* New York, 1969.

Rule, J.C. (ed.) *Louis XIV and the craft of kingship.* Ohio, 1969.

Sainte-Beuve, C.A. *Causeries du lundi,* 8 vols. trans. E.J. Trenchman, London, 1909.

Salmon, J.H.M. *Society in crisis. France in the sixteenth century.* London, 1975.

Schalk, E. *From valor to pedigree: ideas of nobility in France in the sixteenth and seventeenth centuries.* Princeton, New Jersey, 1986.

Shennan, J.H. (ed.), *Government and society in France 1461–1661.* London, 1969.

Taveneaux, R. (ed.), *Jansénisme et politique.* Paris, 1965.

Vovelle, M. *Idéologies and mentalités.* Paris, 1982.

Index

90